ARLEN ROTH
Hot Guitar

Miller
Freeman
Books

San Francisco

Published by Miller Freeman Books
600 Harrison Street, San Francisco, CA 94107
©1996 by Arlen Roth

Distributed to the book trade in the U.S. and Canada by
Publishers Group West,
P.O. Box 8843,
Emeryville, CA 94662

Distributed to the music trade in the U.S. and Canada by
Hal Leonard Publishing,
P.O. Box 13819,
Milwaukee, WI 53213

ISBN 0-87930-276-3

Text design: Brad Greene

Printed in the United States of America

96 97 98 99 6 5 4 3 2 1

un Miller Freeman

Dedication

This book is dedicated to my wife Deborah,
my two daughters (and #1 guitar students) Gillian and Alexis,
and to the memory of my dear friend, Danny Gatton.

Contents

Introduction

This book embodies over 10 years of "Hot Guitar," collecting dozens of lessons and hundreds of licks from the column I wrote for *Guitar Player* magazine from December 1982 through June 1993. I truly enjoyed writing this column, and the reactions I've gotten worldwide have always shown me that I've had a dedicated readership. I also know that it was one column that really had a following, and I always loved how I could take an eclectic approach with it, jumping from country to rock to slide, from blues to R&B to rockabilly, and feel appreciated for it. I've met many students at clinics or concerts who have told me that they saved every single column, and hearing that kind of reaction always made it truly worthwhile.

Quite a few of the artists I've worked with have told me that my own personal sound might be described as flashy. In this book, we will definitely cover the hotter aspects of playing, not only regarding lead styles, but rhythm techniques too. What I've found after years of experience in the studio and onstage with many different types of artists is that a guitarist can modify his playing and adapt it to the requirements of the particular situation while still revealing his own distinctive musical personality. Developing this kind of balance is important, and it's one of the things we'll be discussing in detail. And we won't be concentrating only on the styles of guitarists who've influenced me. We'll also take a look at the contributions of many other important guitarists as well.

I want to thank all of the *Guitar Player* readers out there who have been following me all these years; it's been a blast giving so much to you. I also want to thank everyone at *Guitar Player* who helped me so much, especially Jim Crockett, Tom Wheeler, Tom Mulhern, Dominic Milano, Dan Forte, Matt Kelsey, and Jim Ferguson.

—*Arlen Roth*

Preface

A Conversation with Arlen Roth

More than hot licks

Ironically, everything about Arlen Roth—best known as the author of several method books, the founder of the Hot Licks video series, and a monthly *Guitar Player* columnist for over ten years—spells performer. He may be a respected teacher, but there is nothing academic about this energetic hot-shot from the Bronx.

Roth grew up surrounded by music and the arts. His father, whose penname is Al Ross, comes from the golden age of single-panel cartoonists and is a regular contributor to *The New Yorker* and other magazines. He encouraged Arlen to take up flamenco guitar, so armed with a Favilla classical, the 11-year-old began formal lessons before developing an appetite and an aptitude for rock and roll. Roth enrolled in New York's High School of Music and Art, the school that *Fame* is based on, and studied art and photography while leading a local blues-rock band. In 1971, the 19-year-old moved upstate to Woodstock, where he played regularly with the likes of John Prine, Artie and Happy Traum, John Sebastian, Eric

Actor Ralph Maccio and Arlen Roth shooting *Crossroads* in Mississippi, 1985. Photo: Stephen Vaughn, courtesy Columbia Pictures.

Andersen, and Paul Butterfield, former partner of one of Arlen's first guitar idols, Michael Bloomfield. By 1973, he was playing sessions at New York's A&R studios, owned by producer Brooks Arthur and engineer Phil Ramone (who later produced artists such as Billy Joel, Paul Simon, and Julian Lennon). In 1978, he toured with Art Garfunkel, and in 1979, he fronted Phoebe Snow's group and recorded his first solo LP, *Arlen Roth/Guitarist,* which won Best Instrumental Guitar Performance at the Montreux Jazz Festival in 1979.

In 1983, Roth joined Simon & Garfunkel's reunion-tour band, and in 1985 he received a call from another early idol, Duane Eddy. The King of Twang enlisted Roth's talents (and band) to back him for his first East Coast dates in decades. Roth describes the union as "a marriage made in heaven."

Arlen received another important call in 1985, this time from Ry Cooder. Ry was scoring a film entitled *Crossroads* and needed someone intimately familiar with blues and slide techniques to teach actor Ralph Macchio (star of *The Karate Kid*) to convincingly mime his parts on guitar.

His ever-growing Hot Licks family of artist/instructors now includes such luminaries as Steve Morse, Tal Farlow, Jerry Jemmott, Albert Collins, John Entwistle, James Burton, Joe Pass, Vinnie Moore, Buddy Guy, Otis Rush, Warren Haynes, Duke Robillard, Ronnie Earl, Danny Gatton, Lee Roy Parnell, Emily Remler, Eric Johnson, Stu Hamm, Chuck Rainey, Brian Setzer, and countless more. His latest CD, "Toolin' Around" features duets with friends Danny Gatton, Brian Setzer, Duke Robillard, Jerry Douglas, Albert Lee, Duane Eddy, Sam Bush, and Bill Lloyd.

In *Guitar Player*'s 1986 interview that follows, Roth talks with Dan Forte about his early influences, favorite guitars, teaching philosophy, and main objective: communicating through the guitar.

When did you first take up guitar?

■ Well, I started on classical when I was 11. Then, of course, the Beatles changed all that, and I got an electric. About a week after they came out, I got an Ideal four-pickup guitar and a Stewart amp. I formed a band called the Everpresent. We all combed our hair down and got black matching velours.

Whom did you base your guitar playing on?

■ At that time, I just knew a bunch of licks from the Byrds and the Beatles and Stones and stuff like that. I could play the lick from "The Last Time" [the Rolling Stones, *Out Of Our Heads*, which made me real cool. Chuck Berry I discovered about a year or two later, and then I wanted to *be* Chuck Berry for five years. He was

Arlen Roth with actors Joe Seneca and Joe Morton on location in Mississippi making "Crossroads," 1985. Photo: Juke Logan

the living end for me. Still is, as far as rock and roll goes. Plus, he's the greatest lyric writer of all time, probably. I despised at the time the greasy element in New York that would always say, "Do 'Midnight Hour.'" I hated that whole thing—Long Island vibrato, we called it—because I really wanted to play some clean, crisp stuff. I wanted to hear harmonies. The Byrds really turned me around.

What was your musical training like in high school?

■ A lot of my musical diversion started happening when I hit the High School of Music and Art, because it was a melting pot for the whole city. I was in high school when the blues craze hit. It was like, "Well, who are you? Are you Bloomfield or Kalb?" Well, I was Bloomfield. Butterfield used to tell me that it would give him shivers because I even acted like Bloomfield when I played—and I never saw him play. I idolized the guy. Really, there was a certain period when how Bloomfield went, the world of guitar went. I walked around when I was 14 with a shiny suit and shades, wondering what I was doing here. Because the Bronx was pretty much a musical vacuum. I grew up there in the period of doo-wop stuff on the street corners. But Mike Bloomfield was just so brilliant and so wonderful. He was one of the few players whose stuff I tried to pick right off the record. "Blues With A Feeling" [*The Paul Butterfield Blues Band*]—it took me years to figure out that was a 9th chord; I thought it was a three-note slide. That was a very important developmental period for a lot of guitarists. I was serious about it all along, but at 16 or 17 was when I really blossomed and started forming my own bands. Then I went to the Philadelphia College of Art and started playing with a lot of real country musicians—people from western Pennsylvania, West Virginia, and places like that.

*Was country music very foreign
to you at first?*

■ It actually wasn't because I was unbiased—I would listen to anything. Trends and other people didn't influence me at all, because I knew no one who was interested in music like me. So late at night, I would tune in the radio stations. Even in the Bronx, I would listen to WWVA, the Wheeling West Virginia Jamboree, on a clear night and just soak up that stuff. There was an attitude in New York City about country music, and there still is. There's even an attitude about guitar. I really feel that, quite frankly, New York is not even a good guitar town. It's unfortunate because it made for a lot of years of real difficulty for me in studio work. I was getting a lot of calls, but the work was not what I wanted to play.

*At your age, were you getting the types of calls that,
say, five to seven years earlier would have been for
David Bromberg?*

■ No. I wished! They were the kind of calls that Bucky Pizzarelli or Tony Mottola would get. What happened was, I did do a couple of really hot solos on blues and rock things. So then they assumed, "Wow, this guy can play that stuff so well, imagine what he's like on the other stuff"—which they assume every guitar player knows. So I started subbing a lot for Eric Weissberg on country things on pedal steel. They'd have sheet music in front of me that was ten arms long, and of course I didn't want to look at it. First of all, I couldn't read it; second, I had to look at the steel to stay in tune. One time they did that to me with [actor] Henry Gibson. I had to play all the music from the movie *Nashville*. Luckily, I had just seen the movie, so I remembered the tunes.

*Growing up in New York City and studying guitar in
school, didn't you ever go through a period when you
wanted to play jazz?*

■ That's an interesting question. The answer is no, because jazz turned me off in a certain respect. I would buy records by people like Tony Mottola—the only people I knew then as jazz players. And the kind of music, the tunes and all, put me off as being "older person's music." It sounded like a lounge band to me. I was falling in love with things like country too much to let jazz in. I admired it from afar. But I felt that I had a style to *protect*, in a sense—because it was getting me places. People were saying that I had my own approach, with all the string-bending. I'm assimilating all the time, but jazz just didn't inspire me—the kinds of guitars that were played, the whole thing. It was like night and day to what I really loved: blues.

*Even though you went to the High School of Music and Art,
was all your guitar training self-taught?*

■ That's right. I was an art student at the High School of Music and Art.

Did you ever teach yourself theory and how to read music?

■ I taught myself theory, obviously. I taught myself to write music for my books. When I got the deal to write my first book, *Slide Guitar,* I was only 21. I wrote that on the road, mostly with John Prine. I taught myself how to write the music, and as a result I became better at reading. But I don't practice it anymore. It stands in the way of my learning process. You know—you hear it, you think it, you play it; whereas the music cuts that off right in the middle like a saw. What I do for my books now is run through and—boom—write the tablature almost train-of-thought. After that, I do the music over it, because that's the more tedious part.

*Do you think that for the styles you ordinarily teach—
country, blues, rock, slide—tablature has an advantage
over standard notation?*

■ I really don't know. I still feel that the best way, of course, is listening. I think all the things I put into the tablature I put into the music as well. For example, if the note is bent up and is in parentheses, that's also in the music. I would highly recommend being able to use both, to not have an attitude about either, because you might come across a really cool book where you have to know one or the other.

Can you teach ear training?

■ You can press the right buttons. You can get the person on the right track to believing that they have an ear in the first place. When people say, "Oh, I can't even carry a tune," right away I know that's not true. Everybody has an ear to a certain extent; it's just a question of the right time in your life and the right age that that's tapped and encouraged so you start to recognize things. That, to me, is what ear training is. If I sing a lick, I'm still picturing a guitar fingerboard in my mind because that's how I see music.

*Do you remember when you reached a point where
you could hear a passage of a solo and not have to
trial-and-error every note to figure it out?*

■ That happened right away. In fact, I was able to hear positions. If a guy played a *C* note on the 5th fret of the *G* string, I could tell that it was the *G* string and not the 1st fret of the *B* string. I could hear the subtle, more rounded tone of the *G*. That just seemed to come second nature to me right away because I listened to players who seemed to stick within certain positions—like Bloomfield.

He'd get into a certain position and milk it for all it was worth. Or B.B. King, who would stay in that pentatonic thing and milk that.

Did you ever figure out those patterns, see them repeating themselves, and figure out who played in which ones?

■ Sure.

Did you give them names?

■ Yeah. Right away I started calling them box patterns for the sake of my books and for teaching my students. I knew all the scales and positions already. I discovered these box patterns just out of a need for improvisation, a need to express myself within what I knew. Then I realized that this knowledge could be passed on, and I wrote it out as patterns. I had box patterns in my books and tapes. I think it's a great way of learning. A student can really see that there are areas in which you can explore and feel relatively safe for a while. Be happy with what you know. When I used to know only two or three licks, I was so happy with them. I was able to feel confident with those. As long as you know what you're speaking of. Instead, these days you run across guitar players who can play any scale in the world, but they still don't know what to do with them.

How do you break somebody of those habits, though? It's still possible to hear some very well-known, top-flight players running through their vocabularies, "playing technique."

■ Something has to rub off. They have to have a little bit of a revelation and realize that there is something they are missing. I had a lesson with a student about four years ago. The guy was a fairly accomplished fusion-type player. But, as is the case with a lot of these players, he had no vibrato technique whatsoever. We spent an agonizing day working on one note of vibrato. He said he wasn't leaving until he had it right, because this had been killing him for years. I taught him the whole left-hand pivoting thing, the B.B. King thing. It was a revelation.

Did you ever get into English blues players such as Eric Clapton or Peter Green?

■ Not at all. I didn't know who Peter Green was, and Clapton didn't impress me because, at the time, what he was doing I felt I could already do. The sound of Cream bothered me because it was very muddy, very cloudy. The whole group seemed to be in the same range, and I couldn't discern what was going on. I would rather have heard a crisp Rickenbacker 12-string at that time, or Clarence White. Of course, we're talking '67 or '68. And at that time I would certainly rather listen to B.B. King or Bloomfield than Clapton.

Before Cream, did you get to hear Clapton with John Mayall—like the Bluesbreakers *album?*

■ No. See, when I later heard that, that was great. It had the energy. But, yeah, Cream disturbed me to no end. The *interest* in Cream disturbed me. I really wondered what was going to happen to the guitar. Jimi Hendrix I loved—his soulful things, like "Wind Cries Mary" [*Are You Experienced?*]. I knew this guy was coming from heavy R&B roots that were so sweet. When I finally heard him play straight blues, he was one of the most brilliant musicians ever. I saw him at Woodstock; I sat there in the mud in front. He sent me a lot more at that time than Clapton did. But I must admit, I became very self-involved in my style right away and very cynical of a lot of the music that was going down. So I refused to listen to a lot of what was happening. Certain songs would move me, but there wasn't much guitar playing, except that I listened to my old standbys.

After being immersed in blues, was it much of a detour when you got heavily into country players?

■ To me, it wasn't. It was a chance to be able to help my own style evolve. As far as people saying that I'm playing country licks in a blues song or blues licks in a country song, I like to have that diversion, that unique approach. The country stuff was just a breath of fresh air for me. I did get into the real purist stuff for a while because I had to. I wanted to be able to play Dobro like Bashful Brother Oswald, so I learned all his stuff off Roy Acuff records. I had all these obscure Starday albums that I found in a TV shop in Monticello, New York. I started playing pedal steel in '68, though I gave it up a few years ago because I just couldn't stand lugging it around—plus, I prefer making the *guitar* sound that way. I've never been one to do a lot of miming of a person first, as a means of learning. It was more like, I just have to figure out how he's getting that sound—or at least get an inkling. Of course, my style always evolved, and the equipment changed my style a lot, too—the instruments themselves.

When you finally got a good electric guitar, what was it?

■ I had a Guild Starfire for about a year; I was still playing rhythm then. But in '68, I got my first real good electric guitar; my '52 gold-top Les Paul with a trapeze tailpiece. I had put a deposit on a factory-ordered [Gibson] Byrdland, and, after six months, it came in the wrong finish. They called it a sunburst, but it was just black and yellow—sunstroke [*laughs*]. I picked it up and bent the *B* string up, and the nut broke off the guitar. The salesman gave me the money back, so I went around the corner and tried out that Les Paul. When I played it, that was it.

Arlen Roth and his late friend, Danny Gatton in 1994.
Photo: Tom Gage

How long did you stick with the trapeze tailpiece?

■ The trapeze combination only lasted a year-and-a-half. I had that taken off, and Bill Lawrence, who was working for [store owner/designer] Dan Armstrong, put on a regular tune-o-matic bridge so that I could damp with the heel of my hand. I played that exclusively for four years. In '71, I found my '54 Strat in the trunk of somebody's car in Woodstock. It cost me $75.00. The '54 turned me around. That made me have to play a lot cleaner. I was already playing country on the Les Paul, but the sound wasn't quite right.

There isn't a lot of history of Strats in country music, either.

■ No. And I played a lot of it. I used to play that thing on the treble pickup, too—had a good sound. Then I found my dream-come-true, my '53 Tele. It turned out to be the greatest dream I've ever known.

Did you use the "in-between" position on the Strat pickup selector—the middle and rear pickups together?

■ Yeah, I would balance it up there and just hope it held. Three-position switch, of course. It's ingenious of Mark Knopfler to put a piece of tape across there to automatically get that position, but I wanted the treble possibilities, too. Certain guitars bring out certain things. On the Stratocaster, I love playing those three-note things and those little block pull-offs. They just sound good on that instrument. Of course, now when people hear me play those licks with that tone, they say, "Right, Mark Knopfler," but when "Sultans Of Swing" came out [*Dire Straits*], I had friends call me because they thought I must have been on that session. I'd been playing that style for quite a while. Actually, to me, the Tele sounds the purest. I mean, for single-note stuff and of course the country things—even blues.

Didn't Mike Bloomfield use a Telecaster on
The Paul Butterfield Blues Band *album?*

■ Yeah. I think he used Teles throughout that period—on *East West,* too. The Les Paul was a whole change. The thing I like about the Tele is that you can really play very sweetly with a lot of sustain at lower volumes. If you want to overdub an electric guitar part that's as sweet as an acoustic, you get out the Strat or the Tele. It's more subtle.

There's a lot more definition with a Telecaster.

■ That's the word.

Do you use different guitars for slide because of the tone or the setup?

■ It's generally because of the pickup. Oddly enough, I'm happiest with the '53 Tele for slide right now. The pickup is like a fat Hawaiian guitar. Granted, the action is kind of low, but tuned up to open *E,* the strings are bouncier and higher, so there's no problem. I occasionally use my Les Pauls for slide or the Res-o-glas Nationals for certain funky tones. I also use lap steels a lot. They're the fattest-sounding things in the world. My solos on "Kids On The Block" on *Hot Pickups*—that's my 1930s Rickenbacker Bakelite lap steel. For regular guitar, I've been playing a Guild Nightbird a lot lately; it's unbelievable. Also, I've got several ESPs. The custom-made ones with my name on the headstock are based on a Tele, but with a solid body shaped like a National map-shape. They have a [Gibson] Firebird humbucker in the neck position, a Strat pickup in the middle, and a Tele lead pickup.

Do you use a variety of amps for different sounds?

■ For my albums, I bring in the '64 Fender Deluxe Reverb and a '63 Vox AC-30. I just found a '58 Fender Tremolux

that was never played, never un-wrapped. It's beautiful, but I haven't used it yet on anything. Sometimes I use a Fender Twin, if I want to get a very clean sound, and also a Jim Kelley. The Jim Kelly was perfect on the Simon & Garfunkel tour because when it was quiet, it was clean and sweet, and when I wanted to really crank, it had natural distortion. I'm looking forward to using the Seymour Duncan amp as well. When I tried it out, Seymour just put together a setup that he said would be my sound, and damn if he wasn't right—because Seymour comes from a Deluxe Reverb school, too. I like things to be a little fatter now than just the Deluxe.

Arlen Roth and James Burton performing at the Danny Gatton Benefit concert in NYC, 1995. Photo: Tom Gage

Since you got away from taking bits and pieces from different players and started coalescing a style, have you been pretty much on the same track?

■ That's a tough question. Of course I'm on the same track because I'm the same person—one track. Yeah, it's been a development of my style, completely. It hasn't been, like, "Now I'd like to master Doc Watson's style," or whoever. I can write about these people's styles because I know a little bit about what makes them tick. But at some point, I really went full-steam ahead on my own approach, my own style.

One of the really distinctive elements of your style is that you stay close to the melody, but you constantly embellish around it. Does that come from accompanying vocalists?

■ I've never thought about it before, but it probably does. I always thought that the concept of stating a melody and then having to embellish upon it was a rather old and worn-out thing, but I found a real love in it. Because it forces you to expose what your language is—the way you really hear something. Now I'm getting into a groove with it. "Unchained Melody" [*Lonely St.*] is just perfect for it; it's really emotional. Embellishing upon a theme is something that I continue to work on, and I'm trying to simplify even more. I'm trying to say more with fewer notes.

Is it hard for you to hold back, to play less?

■ Not anymore. It was when I was younger. Now I'm very hip to the fact that when you're playing the melody, you are still showing your approach and your tone and your texture and your phrasing—even in playing something that people have heard a thousand times before. You're still doing it your way. And I can see that people

appreciate that. They appreciate just listening to something that sounds pretty. And then, when they hear you taking it around the corner and twisting it a little bit, the smiles start, and we're communicating. Whenever I'm soloing, the theme, the melody of the song, is always paramount. I like the speed only for the bursts of when I'm feeling it, not like some trumpet player trying to reach the highest note at the end of every song. That doesn't work for me.

Can you have the same attitude when soloing, with or without an audience?

■ I need an audience—just need to know that there's another soul out there, someone who's being communicated to. I generally don't do a great solo in the studio until somebody happens to walk in—and as far as I'm concerned, the more, the merrier. Like most people, I'm more nervous playing for three people in my living room than I would be for 100,000 people in the darkness. That need to communicate is so important. It's not enough to be recording and to know that somebody out there sometime is going to be listening to the record. I'm generally a first-take guy. Like "When A Man Loves A Woman" [*Hot Pickups*]—that's a first take, straight through.

When you're playing an off-the-cuff solo, do you ever think of the technical devices that you're using?

■ No. I must admit that I'm guilty of that when I'm performing for a seminar audience, because I realize that they're looking strictly at technique and wanting to know what I'm doing with my hands. But when I'm just playing, no, I don't go through that thought process. The thought process is much more from the heart. It just sort of happens.

You're just sort of hearing it in your head and playing it, without having to decipher it first?

■ Exactly. Hear it, and go for it. Because, if you say, "I'm going to use this technique or that technique," nine times out of ten, you're going to fall back on something you're a little safe with. And I definitely don't try to do that.

Philosophy aside, are there physical things you do on the guitar that other players don't?

■ [*Plays a pedal steel-like lick, holding the D string stationary, while bending the G string a whole-step and the A string a half-step in the opposite direction.*] Those are among my more original things—double bends. Keep in mind that you don't have to really worry about one bend being a whole-step and the other a half-step; the different gauges take care of that, and you bend with the same pressure for each finger. I really pride myself in probably being technically the most proficient slide player around. I mean, I don't think there's a cleaner slide player in the book, really. I hate to sound boastful, but I think I have a unique approach to slide, in being very clean and exacting with my technique. It's almost like what a Hawaiian guitar player would do. Of course, a guitar player's phrasing is something that's so much his own. I like to juxtapose open strings with the fingerpicking technique. I try not to think of scales and that kind of stuff. I picture it more with shapes and substitutions.

When you got into playing pedal steel-like things on guitar, did it grow out of listening to steel players, or from listening to other guitarists who would also imitate steel?

■ All three. It first grew out of a love for Hawaiian guitar, and trying to imitate that.

Did you adopt your flatpick-and-fingers style knowing that other people, such as James Burton, played that way?

■ I didn't know who Burton was. I was very very naive about stuff like that. That was before my time, in a lot of ways. I did it out of necessity, trying to get these steel licks separated. It's great because you can *grab* the notes. You're getting all three or four notes at the same time.

When did you start your Hot Licks instruction tapes?

■ I began formulating the thing in '79. I recorded most of the tapes when I was doing a soundtrack for a movie about Robert Johnson, but the movie was never released. It's a shame, because I'm really proud of it. I

consider it to be easily my best playing. It wasn't as if it's Robert Johnson doing it—it's all interpretations. In fact, a lot of it's electric. A lot of it is Chicago blues era. (Note: this album was finally released as a CD called *Incarnation* in 1994.)

Do you think it's odd that you started the Hot Licks instruction series, involving cassettes and written music, even though you were self-taught and, as you said, never copied things note-for-note?

■ It's much deeper than that. There was something I knew I had to teach, but the lessons are informal. I'm allowed to go off on tangents and let my mind wander—just like a real good lesson. But the end product is a self-teaching method, and you want to help that student open up doors for himself. It's not structured at all—you read it, you hear it, you play it. There are a few things you can read, but most of it is very descriptive and very organic. Of course, now that I'm a publisher, the different series become as individual as the different artists teaching them. In other words, Steve Morse's course is much more studious and regimented—just the way he is. With me, I wanted to put my learning process down on tape for people to understand the way I learn—including a couple of little asides and stories and hints that you could pass along. But the idea is, it's a new way of learning. It doesn't put people off.

So you're more into teaching sort of an attitude and a concept instead of, "Here's a Don Rich lick."

■ In the long run, that's right. I'll say, "This is reminiscent of what Clarence White played," or I'll explain how I evolved from the Clarence White style. You've got to give them something specific. But the idea is to encourage, to push their playing in *their* direction.

Does it matter if some of the other artist/teachers in the series have a completely different teaching philosophy?

■ Not at all. I choose them because I respect them and because they have something to say. I want the tapes to be as unique as *they* are.

It's odd that you have such notoriety as an educator and an author, yet your attitude seems to be directed toward performance.

■ Yeah. You hit it on the head. I'm a performer first, and I always will be. You can't change that in somebody. I think that's what makes my stuff very communicative; it's done on a performance level. Like when I play at my seminars, I get very emotional. Teaching is the same high.

Notational Symbols

■ The following symbols are used in this book to indicate fingerings, techniques, and effects commonly used in guitar music notation. Keep in mind that certain symbols are found in either the tab or the standard notation only—not both.

4● Left-hand fingering is designated by small Arabic numerals near note heads (1=first finger, 2=second finger, 3=third finger, 4=little finger, and t=thumb).

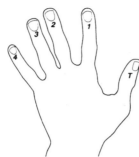

p● Right hand fingering designated by letters (*p*=thumb, *i*=index, *m*=middle, *a*=ring, and *c*=little [or *l*=pinky]).

②● A circled number (1-6) indicates the string on which a particular note is to be played.

⊓ Pick downstroke.

V Pick upstroke.

CV The C indicates a full barre; the Roman numeral designates the proper fret.

¢V The ¢ indicates a 1st finger half-barre covering either the first three or four strings, depending on what is called for in the notation.

3[Partial barre with the designated finger.

〜 Left-hand finger vibrato.

B
7(9) Bend; play the first note and bend to the required pitch (bent note is in parentheses). See tab explanation.

R
(9)7 Reverse bend; strike an already bent note, then allow it to return to its unbent pitch (bent note is in parentheses).

H
7 9 Hammer-on (lower note to higher).

P
9 7 Pull-off (higher note to lower).

② Indicates right-hand tapping technique.

S
3/5 Slide; play first note and slide to the next pitch (in tab, an upward slide is indicated with an upward-slanting line, while a downward slide is indicated with a downward-slanting line).

↕ Strum (an arrowhead is often used to indicate direction).

ras
Rasgueado.

//// Indicated desired rhythm for chordal accompaniment (the choice of voicings is up to the player).

How tablature works

■ The horizontal lines represent the guitar's strings, the top line standing for the high *E*. The numbers designate the frets to be played. For instance, a 2 positioned on the first line would mean to play the second fret on the first string (0 indicates an open string). Time values are indicated on the coinciding lines of standard notation seen directly above the tablature. Read tablature from left to right in the conventional manner.

Chord diagrams

■ In all chord diagrams, vertical lines represent the strings, and horizontal lines represent the frets. The following symbols are used:

—— Nut; indicates first position.

x Muted string, or string not played.

o Open string.

⌒ Barre (partial or full).

● Placement of left-hand fingers.

III Roman numerals indicate the fret at which a chord is located.

1 Arabic numerals indicate left-hand fingering (1=index, etc.)

CHAPTER ONE

Getting Started

Rhythmic notation

■ Before diving into our first musical examples, let's talk a little bit about rhythmic notation. For starters, we'll be working in 4/4 time, which means that each measure, or bar, has four beats, and that the quarter note is the basic unit of the beat (in other words, one beat, or one foot-tap, equals a quarter note).

Now, there are several accepted methods of counting and notating these beats and their possible subdivisions. In this series we'll use those conventions my students and I have found to be easiest to grasp and most relevant to the guitar player. Here, then, is the basic vocabulary of notes we'll be using.

A *whole note* is a single note that, by itself, fills up an entire measure of 4/4 time; that is, it's four beats long. The four beats are numbered below the staff; here, the note is played on beat one and held all the way through beat four. The *half note* has a duration of two beats. Here, the first half note is struck on count one and held through count two; the second half note is played on count three and held through count four. The *quarter note* has a duration of one beat, or a single count. Here, we're playing four quarter notes in all, one on each of the four beats. Practice Ex. 1 thoroughly.

Continuing in the direction of slicing smaller and smaller pieces of the pie, we'll now begin to subdivide the beat itself into parts, playing *more than one note per beat*. In the following example, we are playing two notes per beat, or eight notes in all. We'll have to modify our count now to cover those between-the-beat (offbeat) notes. Easily done—we just use the word "and" for the second half of each beat. But remember, even though we're counting "one-and, two-and, three-and, four-and" in the next example, we're still playing the "one, two, three," and "four" right in time with the foot-taps, at exactly the same rate, or *tempo* as before. Ex. 2 shows another way to look at it—watch your foot tap as you count, and say "and" as your foot comes up.

Finally, let's divide each of the four beats into three parts, each part being called a *triplet*. Here things get slightly tricky. You can think of each beat as a three syllable word, if you like—"*Mex*-i-co, *Mex*-i-co, *Mex*-i-co," for

example. But how to count it? Some teachers will verbalize "*one*-an-a, *two*-an-a," etc. I prefer the following method: "*one*-two-three, *two*-two-three, *three*-two-three, *four*-two-three." The important thing is to stress the beat and maintain the tempo (Ex. 3).

For the time being, we'll be working within these relatively straightforward, uncomplicated note values so you can concentrate more on getting your technique together. However, as the book progresses, we'll be getting into increasingly subtle, interesting, and intricate licks. (Moral: Learn these early lessons well.)

Ex. 1

Ex. 2

Ex. 3

Combining hammer-ons & pull-offs

■ Now on to one of the hotter elements of guitar playing—the ability to combine hammer-ons and pull-offs for added left-hand speed in lead guitar.

Often when we hear the repetitious riffing of some ear-crushing showboat, it is more likely than not the result of a heavy-handed combination of these two techniques. But while some people use them to excess, when employed tastefully they are vital parts of the repertoire of any lead player. I'll define hammers and pulls more clearly so we can all begin with the same degree of understanding.

The *hammer-on*, indicated by an arch between two notes with an "h" over it, is simply any finger "hammering-on" to a second note (on a higher fret), after the initial note is picked. The force of the hammer stroke causes a second note to be sounded—in effect giving new life to the string. To attack the string, the hammer-on finger shouldn't be too far above the fingerboard. Using more strength within closer quarters like this increases left-hand agility and control.

The *pull-off* technique is generally the opposite of the hammer-on (note that it's indicated by an arch with a "p" over it). To play Ex. 4, pre-position both fingers of your left hand. Pluck the *G* with your right hand and cause the *E* to sound by pulling away the finger positioned on the *G*. Remember that pull-offs sound stronger when you remove your finger from the fretboard at approximately a 45° angle, while slightly catching the string with your callus.

To get a better idea of what hammers and pulls should feel like together, try playing Ex. 5 using only the left hand. The second hammer-on is stronger than the other two because the hammered note is on the beat (the other hammer-ons go to offbeat notes). Other than that, maintain an even volume. This is precisely how flashy players are able to play with one hand—connecting a hammer-on to a pull-off.

Ex. 4

Ex. 5

Hammer-ons & pull-offs in a blues scale

■ Guitarists are lucky to have an instrument on which so many of the major building blocks of music make such memorable visual patterns. Chords, arpeggios, and scales all have their fretboard images. Rock guitarists are particularly fortunate because one of their most important scale patterns—a mainstay in the solo work of artists like B.B. King, Eric Clapton, or Eddie Van Halen—is especially easy to see, to finger, and to memorize. Before going any further let's pause and consider this indispensable rock and blues scale pattern. Then let's put it to use.

Ex. 6

➤

Many of you will already be familiar with the diagram in Ex. 6. Note how the first finger never needs to leave the vicinity of the 5th fret; you don't have to stretch for any of the notes—they all fall within a natural, four-fret, four-finger span. Now see how the written notes in Ex. 7 correspond to this fretboard pattern. These notes form a pentatonic (five-tone) blues scale in the key of *A*. (A comment about distinguishing the *A* blues scale from the *A* major scale: the former includes the *C* and *G*—the "blue" notes—while in the latter scale the corresponding notes are *C#* and *G#*.)

We'll have many more occasions to use this scale in the lessons to come. Right now we're going to employ it as we pick up the discussion of hammer-ons and pull-offs.

It's only when you start to combine other strings and move freely between them that you see the true advantages of hammer-ons and pull-offs used in tandem. This scale, which I often refer to as the "backtrack," uses hammers and pulls in combination while the index finger makes some rather rapid shifts across the strings. Why call it the backtrack scale? Though the general motion of the notes is down, there are a couple of skips back up in each measure. See if you can reverse the pattern and create an *ascending* backtrack scale (Ex. 8).

The possibilities these techniques offer are endless, so I'll cap this off with some of the hotter runs that can be derived from this particular blues scale. Let's look at the four examples in greater detail. In Ex. 9 you have a difficult leap from the *E* on the second string to the *D* on the fifth string (sixth and seventh notes). Learn to make the jump quickly with the index finger in order to maintain the tempo. In Ex. 10 there is a *short* barre across the first and second strings only. When you come to the *D#* (a passing tone commonly added to the five-note blues scale), get the 3rd and 1st fingers ready, pinning the 7th and 5th frets while you're picking the 8th fret *D#*. Be sure to change your time feeling to two notes to the beat instead of three when you come to the third example. Ex. 11 presents no special problems—try playing it over and over, gradually increasing your speed to the limit.

Please keep practicing, not only because more hot stuff awaits you, but because each lesson is going to demand a little more of your technique and musicianship.

Ex. 7

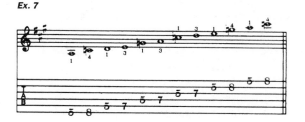

Ex. 8

Ex. 9

Ex. 10

Ex. 11

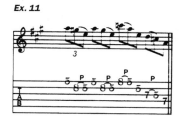

Left-hand roll licks

■ One of my favorite methods for developing left-hand speed is through what I like to call "roll" licks. These are certain licks and runs requiring a smooth combination of hammer-ons, pull-offs, and partial barre positions. "Roll" describes the effect of sequences of equal valued notes, frequent hammer-ons and pull-offs, and a limited number of picked strings. Bear in mind that when you *are* picking, a subtle application of up and down strokes will add an even smoother roll to the licks. If you're using a pick-and-finger approach to lead guitar, you should have an even easier time with these roll licks (more on the pick and fingers technique in a later column).

The use of partial barres for licks obviously necessitates a "closed" position higher up the neck, somewhat of a challenging place to get started on a new technique. For this reason, we'll work with the open position first. The barres are not necessary here, yet you can get the feel of the "roll" from the use of hammer-ons and pull-offs.

The lick in Ex. 12 moves up, then rolls back down to its original starting note. Don't forget to keep strict time and to give each note the same time value.

Ex. 13 involves a hammer-on to *G#*, the 3rd of the *E* major chord (this lick would be applicable only to that chord).

Many new possibilities arise from beginning the licks on the higher strings and working your way down, as the following run illustrates. Note that the hammer-on on the first string is four frets in length, and make sure that your pull-offs are truly left-hand *plucks* that give strong resonance to the string (Ex. 14).

In Ex. 15 and 16 we see how roll licks work in a closed position with a partial barre. These two may be a bit more difficult than the open positions, so practice them slowly at first, working toward synchronization of right and left hands.

Ex. 12

Ex. 13

Ex. 14

Ex. 15

Ex. 16

Hammer-on & pull-off chords for pedal steel effects

■ When I toured with Simon and Garfunkel in 1983, I had to employ many techniques and approaches in each of the 26-song shows. Luckily I was given the chance to be rather interpretive in my own way on quite a few of the tunes. Here's a technique for hammering on and pulling off *chords* to achieve country-flavored pedal steel guitar sounds, which I used on the Simon and Garfunkel classic "Homeward Bound."

On this song, I made considerable use of double hammers and pulls while changing from an *E* to an *A* chord at the ninth position (see Ex. 17). Note that, in effect, this is part of a *G* to *C* chord change transposed from the open position up nine frets: a partial barre copies the form of the open strings (which form *G* when open, *E* at the 9th fret), while the 2nd and 3rd fingers hammer on with part of a *C* chord formation (*A* in the position shown). Study Ex. 17, and you'll see what I mean. Use your 1st finger to barre the second, third, and fourth strings at the 9th fret, and then hammer on with the 2nd finger at the 10th fret of the second string, and the 3rd finger at the 11th fret of the fourth string.

Now we'll elaborate on the idea a little by "rolling" the notes as we hammer on (see Ex. 18). This can be done using a pick, fingers, or a combination of both. The combination approach is ideal, but if you choose to play any of these licks with a flatpick or your fingers alone, it should work out just fine. On the final beat in Ex. 18, the 2nd and 3rd fingers pull off. The delayed pull-off of the 3rd finger (*C#* to *B*) may require some extra concentration on your part at first—just aim for two simultaneous notes on the third beat.

Providing we've created enough sustain with our barre and a good, strong pull-off, we can *slide* the 1st finger down to the 7th fret without plucking the strings again (see Ex. 19). The partial barre at the 7th fret is a *D* chord, so we've managed to make *three* chords (*A, E,* and *D*) while picking only once with the right hand.

These licks come together in my interpretation of the chorus to "Homeward Bound." The lick starts with some hammer-ons and pull-offs within the movable *C* chord formation (again, *A* at the ninth position) before the full chord movements begin. This comes under the category of "roll" licks.

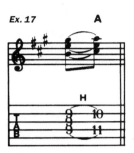

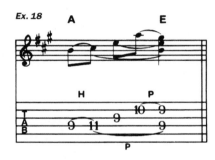

Using the pick & fingers together

■ I've been recommending the combined use of pick and fingers for a long time, especially when a delicate, country-like touch is required. Of course, this doesn't limit the effectiveness this method can have when applied to blues or rock, particularly if your nails can take it!

The advantages of using pick and fingers together are many. First, proper right-hand damping becomes almost second nature because whatever type of lick is being played, the pick and fingers are either in the process of playing the strings or resting on them. The damping will occur more naturally than, say, a situation in which only a flatpick is used, necessitating the use of the heel of your hand to cut off the notes. The photo shows a typical "ready," or damped, position when using the pick and fingers on three adjacent strings.

Another great advantage to this technique is that rather than *dragging* across a chord with a pick you can now *grab* three notes simultaneously, creating a much more accurate, almost piano-like attack. You then have the added option of stopping the very same notes with the same pick and fingers.

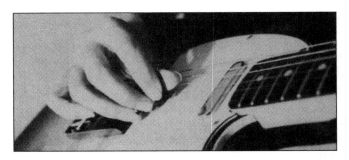

Ex. 20 illustrates the kind of partial chord forms that can be grabbed with the pick and two fingers. Perhaps this technique's major benefit lies in its ability to create rather complex picking patterns that can be translated into numerous positions, which could barely be executed with a flatpick alone.

In the banjo-like exercise in Ex. 21 we learn to use the pick for the hammer-on on the *D* string and the open *G*, while the in-between "drone" notes on the *B* and *E* strings are played consistently with the middle and ring fingers, respectively. You can also try breaking out of this pattern

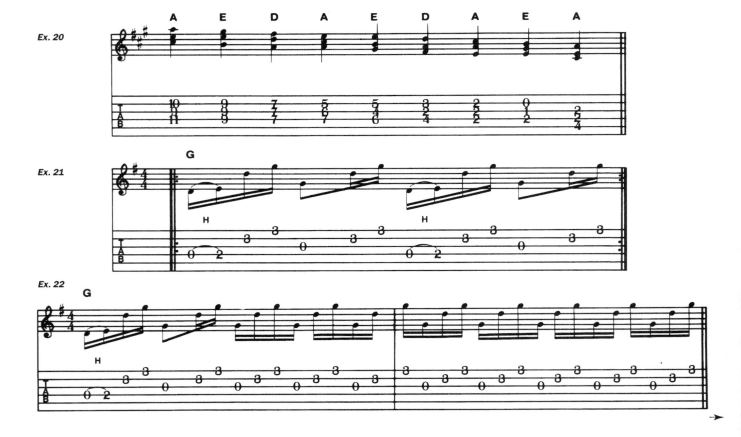

→

by going into a syncopated three-string run, as illustrated in Ex. 22.

Please remember, it'll take some time for you to develop the proper independence between pick and fingers, so don't be too discouraged at first. The sole purpose of these exercises is to help you in developing this style, so stick with them. Keep practicing hard, and try to incorporate these new ideas into your own playing; you just might surprise yourself!

Developing educated ears

■ Rock, blues, country, and jazz guitar styles are largely self-taught. Rather than taking lessons, I spent countless hours better acquainting myself with my instrument because I loved playing. Over the course of my learning experience, I noticed myself gradually assimilating theory while I was picking up licks and techniques. In other words, I learned the "primitive way"; by that I mean through putting two and two together. My knowledge came from seeing how the various fingerboard positions relate to one another and why notes and chords sound the way they do.

I can recall many recording sessions where I had to spontaneously build an unfamiliar chord written on a chart. If a part calls for an *Em9*, you should be able to build it by knowing its basic components—a minor triad with a lowered 7th and a 9th. And once you know the notes of a particular chord, you should be able to find its inversions up and down the fingerboard. Needless to say, if I have to find a new chord under pressure in the studio, it becomes permanently etched in my mind.

I learned as much as I did because I was able to hear the relationships between notes. If you have a fairly good ear, these relationships should become increasingly apparent with time. Eventually you'll find your theoretical knowledge growing in leaps and bounds.

One useful bit of theory for the self-taught musician is knowing the various ways numbers designate chord and note relationships. You've probably heard of a I IV V blues or a I VI II V turnaround. Roman numerals quickly indicate chord progressions. This facilitates communication between musicians and is indispensable in rapidly learning new tunes. A couple of years ago, I was called to do a rather unusual record date that really tested my ability to learn tunes quickly. A few other session players and I recorded an album with the great gospel singer Marion Williams. Since the budget was small, I had to learn the changes to 12 songs in one three-hour date so I could overdub on a solo track she had done. We listened to the cuts once, and with pads and pencils in hand, we took down the changes like secretaries taking dictation. Using Roman numerals made things a lot easier, since the relationship between chords is the same regardless of key.

Roman numerals correspond to the notes of a major scale, which in turn correspond to a chord having the same name as each scale tone. For instance, a I II III IV V progression in the key of *E* would translate to *E, F♯, G♯, A, B*. Many early blues and rock and roll tunes use the I, IV, and V chords in a 12-bar structure. For easy reference, Ex. 23 provides a list of all major keys and their respective I, IV, and V chords. Practice the I IV V progression in all keys, and notice how each combination sounds.

The I VI II V progression is commonly used in ragtime and jazz, and is frequently employed as a turnaround in certain forms of the blues. Ex. 24 shows a table of I VI II V progressions in all keys:

Ex. 23

I	IV	V
C	F	G
C♯	F♯	G♯
D	G	A
D♯	G♯	A♯
E	A	B
F	A♯	C
F♯	B	C♯
G	C	D
G♯	C♯	D♯
C	F	G
A♯	D♯	E
B	E	F♯

Ex. 24

I	VI	II	V
C	A	D	G
C♯	A♯	D♯	G♯
D	B	E	A
D♯	C	F	A♯
E	C♯	F♯	B
F	D	G	C
F♯	D♯	G♯	C♯
G	E	A	D
G♯	F	A♯	D♯
A	F♯	B	E
A♯	G	C	F
B	G♯	C♯	F♯

➤

Ex. 25 is a *C* blues progression featuring the I VI II V turnaround. See if you can play through it with a straight four feel, the way a jazz guitarist might.

Perhaps the most important aspect of knowing chord relationships is being able to recognize a progression by hearing it. Just as in the record date I described earlier, a working guitarist needs to be familiar with all types of chord progressions. Whether you're composing, arrang-

ing, improvising, or learning, you'll benefit by having a solid grasp of theory. I recommend playing through some of your favorite tunes or changes, and learning them in terms of Roman numerals. Next practice recognizing the progressions by ear (listen for familiar sequences on records or the next time you go to a concert). Learning to listen is the key (no pun intended).

Ex. 25

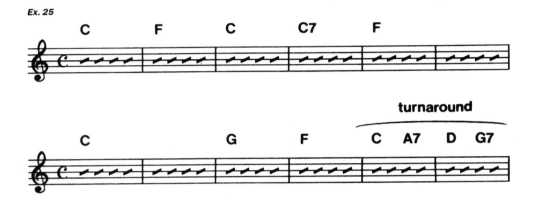

Leads and Solos

Combining string bending with single-note work

■ Let's look at something rarely discussed, but absolutely essential to all types of lead playing—the technique of getting in and getting out of a bending position. Although few have mastered it, this skill is essential to developing the emotional content of one's lead work.

While many jazz stylists employ very subtle bends, most rock and blues players desire a more radical effect, bending a note up a half-step, a whole-step, or even more. In such cases, the fingers alone are not enough. The left *hand* itself must be totally committed to the bending process.

There are two factors that go into this left-hand commitment. First, your thumb *should* come up over the edge of the fingerboard to give some opposing pressure for the bend to work against; second, you should place any other available fingers *behind* the bend to help it along and to push the other strings out of the way. When bending a string down, away from you, the thumb over the fingerboard can still be useful, but it is not as crucial. As you make the bend, your hand should pivot from the point where the base of the index finger presses against the side of the neck.

Ex. 1

Normally, getting out of a bend presents little difficulty. But sometimes a finger tied up in pushing a string will be needed elsewhere for normal fretting. In that case, remove the finger you need while the remaining fingers reinforce the bent note enough to keep it from losing its pitch prematurely. Let's say, for instance, that the 1st, 2nd, and 3rd fingers are involved when you need the 1st finger to play a note on another string. While the 1st finger moves, the 2nd and 3rd fingers remain in firm control of the bent string, and can still sustain, release, or alter the note in any way desired.

The rock/blues solo in Ex. 1 contains several situations calling for sustaining the bend while moving another finger. You should probably do a little experimenting to see whether the 2nd or 3rd finger would be more comfortable in each situation. I know that if I must make a completely independent bend, especially at the start of a lick, I'll always go to the three-finger position. If the bend occurs more *during* the course of a lick, I'm often forced to go to the slightly weaker two-finger approach. (Notes in parentheses are reached by either bending or releasing the previous tone.) Again, you should try each case a few different ways to see which is best suited for you. In a later chapter, we'll be taking a much deeper look into the possibilities—both technical and emotional—which can be achieved through the art of string bending.

Taking off into a solo

■ From the very first note, the soloing guitarist sets the stage for the development and eventual culmination of his musical ideas. (I have also found this to be true in backup situations when great emphasis is placed on fills and answer lines.) From start to finish, you take full responsibility for your guitaristic actions, and for this reason the opening notes of your solo are of paramount importance—like the opening line of a conversation or a public speech.

In previous lessons we've worked with hammer-ons, pull-offs, and string-bending techniques. These three will come into play here, with the addition of yet another important technique—that of *sliding* to a note. An expressive tool for the lead guitarist, sliding also enables one to shift positions rapidly and smoothly.

There are basically two types of slides. The first occurs between two notes with set time values such as the two eighth-notes in Ex. 2.

Sometimes the slide is ornamental—just a quick lead-in with no written time value. In that case start two or three frets below the written note, and rapidly slide into it on the beat (Ex. 3).

Ex. 2

Ex. 3

Ex. 4

Ex. 5

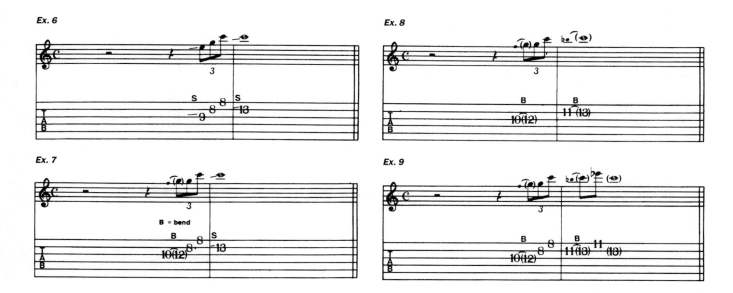

The art of taking off into a solo is certainly one area of guitar playing where the slide can be used to great advantage. A lot of players whose mastery of this technique first knocked me out were among the Chicago-style blues greats. Artists such as Buddy Guy, B.B. King, Freddie King, and Otis Rush helped to perfect the concept of the fantastically fiery and stylish takeoff. Ex. 4, 5 and 6 show three great takeoff licks I love to use in the blues and rock idioms; they are strongly influenced by the styles of B.B. King and Buddy Guy. Please note the combined use of hammer-ons, two-string bars, and slides (the bars should occur only on the first and second strings).

Now in a slightly more difficult vein, we combine string-bending with these takeoff licks. Ex. 7, 8 and 9 are more reminiscent of the playing of Freddie King, Otis Rush, and the English rockers they influenced—Eric Clapton, Jimmy Page, and Mick Taylor (just to name a few). These examples also show a more *intense* solo- or song-starting statement. Again, remember to use the 1st-finger two-string bars only when truly necessary.

Bear in mind that all these licks can be used as fills, too—they're simply better known as intros to songs and solos. Try practicing them slowly at first, gradually building speed as your ability permits. Remember, it can be just as effective to play these licks in a slow situation as in an up-tempo one. You should also try to think up some lead-ins of your own, and experiment with what your *next* musical statement will be after you've taken off into your solo.

Negotiating the I-IV change

■ Taking off into a blues-rock solo is indeed an important moment to a lead guitarist, but where to *next?* So many guitarists complain of simply feeling stuck somewhere on the neck, not knowing what to do except to fall back on the same old licks and scales. Well, hold on; there *is* help.

In most blues situations your opening statement will be on the tonic, or I chord, with the IV chord following quickly thereafter. Some fast thinking is required at the point where the I gives way to the IV (C to F, for example). You must be ready with some subtle alterations in the blues scale to suit this new chord; at the same time you've got to maintain the melodic flow set in motion by the opening statement. Sometimes adapting to the IV chord means an entire shift in position; other times it may mean only a minor change within the pattern you are already playing. (What you do depends on your confidence and willingness to explore uncharted territory.)

The creative picture can be enhanced by understanding how the change in harmony (I-IV) affects the quality of each of the scale tones. Consider $E\flat$ in a C blues scale for example. As the flatted 3rd over the tonic (C), $E\flat$ now has a very tangy sound. At the I-IV change $E\flat$ takes on a new identity—it now becomes the $\flat$7th of the IV chord. So in the key of C, the IV chord—F—is spelled $F, A, C, E\flat$ (that is 1, 3, 5, $\flat$7).The note is still bluesy in this context, but since it has gained a certain stability in its new harmonic role, its melodic flavor, too, has been altered.

Like $E\flat$, the note A can fill various functions within the C blues scale. Over the I chord it forms a 6th (or 13th when the 7th is present), while in the IV chord it functions as the 3rd. Both 3rds and 7ths are excellent harmonic points to emphasize in your solos, so this gives us part of the answer to the question, "Where to next?" The answer, in the case of I-IV in a C blues would be, "You can't go wrong with $E\flat$ and A."

The run in Ex. 10 illustrates how one may subtly target these new notes within the confines of a single scale position.

In Ex. 11 we see how we can drop down below the blues scale we've just played, reaching a position where A and $E\flat$ are accessible in a new range. The alternate fingerings allow the creation of new melodic designs as well.

The same 3rd and 7th chord notes can also be found in a major pentatonic scale form *above* the location of our home-base blues scale. The tonic, C, is in the same spot on the fourth string; however, due to the change in position, it now is fretted with the 1st finger rather than the 3rd (Ex. 12).

In Ex. 13 we take a longer excursion from the home-base pattern used in the intro lick, up to what I call the "B.B. King box position." Here we find a wealth of possibilities, some of the best of which start with a 2nd-finger slide right into the 3rd of the IV chord (A at the 14th fret). Note the new locations of both the 7th ($E\flat$) and the 3rd (A) in this lick.

Bending is also a great tool to use in the execution of IV chord licks. A half-step bend into the IV's $\flat$7th can be especially tasty (Ex. 14).

Try to experiment and expand upon the ideas here, especially in improvisational situations. You may just surprise yourself.

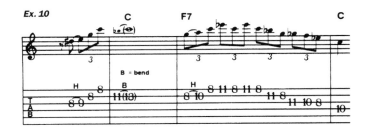

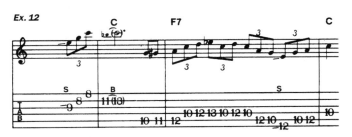

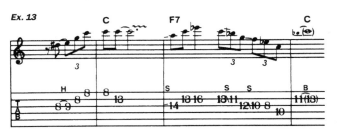

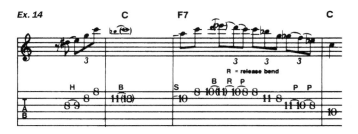

Hot hybrid: Bends with barres

Through combining string bending with partial barre forms, the lead guitarist can produce a variety of exciting licks. What does this hybrid technique have going for it? Well, the barre (or "bar") creates a firm platform from which a great many hammer-ons and pull-offs can be executed, and—given proper picking—you can make many of these licks rather fast and flashy sounding.

Now, the act of getting in and out of a bending position is very important to the proper execution of this type of lick. This is because your left-hand fingers have a dual involvement. In order to commit the *entire* left hand to the bend, they must all push together—and yet they must be instantly available, either for fretting new notes or switching to a partial barre position. All this requires some pretty agile movement on your part and a sense of knowing where you're going ahead of time.

In the first lick (Ex. 15), be sure to commit your entire hand to the bending process, releasing the bend just in time to use your index finger for the barre on the 8th fret of the first and second strings.

The next lick (Ex. 16) is essentially the same as the first, except that we've added a bend from $B\flat$ to C on the last note. Try to use the same three-fingered approach for both bends (back up the bending finger with two others).

In Ex. 17, we play a harmony note with the bend. The harmony note, a high $E\flat$ on the first string, 11th fret, is held by the 4th finger of the left hand. Since we are using the left-hand pinky, we can still afford to invest three fingers in making a strong, clean bend.

The next two examples feature the more difficult sorts of licks associated with this technique. You've probably heard similar sounds in the flashy solos and fills of people like Jimmy Page, Eric Clapton, Jeff Beck, and Jimi Hendrix. These one-bar exercises—as brief as they are—will become quite effective when you are able to play them fast and in quick repetition. Ex. 18 will not require a barre, since we're only playing one string after the bend. When you really get going at a good clip, you'll probably find it easier to use only the 2nd finger for the bend, meanwhile keeping the index finger firmly planted on the second string at the 8th fret.

Ex. 19 is rather difficult to execute cleanly, mainly because the hammer-on that crosses the first and second beats is delayed, occurring after the intervening C has sounded. In other words, the second-string G must sustain long enough to receive the hammer-on $B\flat$ after the first string C has been plucked. Just to be sure we understand, let's analyze the fretboard events: on notes one and two of the third beat, pick the third-string F and bend it up to G and allow it to ring as you go into the

Ex. 15

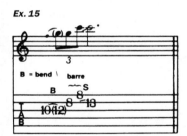

Ex. 16

Ex. 17

Ex. 18

Ex. 19

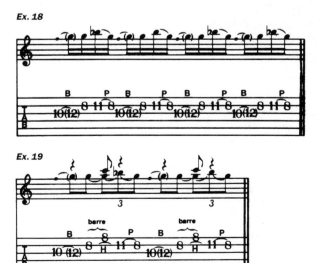

→

triplet. On the first note of the triplet, pick the first-string *C,* and on the *second* note, hammer-on *B♭* from the still-ringing *G* on the second string. For the third note of the triplet, pull off from the 11th fret to the 8th fret. Clear? If not, try playing one note at a time, while reviewing the instructions as you go. It should click then. Once you understand the example, gradually build up speed. Once again, you'll probably find that your best bet for achieving maximum speed is a 2nd-finger bend under a firmly mounted barre.

Rock soloing on the lower strings

■ Here's an oft-requested but not oft-taught guitar technique: using the lower strings in rock solos. The majority of guitar soloing seems to take place on the top three strings. There's nothing wrong with this—quite the contrary. Often a lead instrument, the guitar can better be distinguished from the rhythm section by using the treble strings. Even old-timey acoustic fingerpickers would usually play the melody line on top while maintaining a bass drone or alternation with the thumb.

But I have also found the lower strings to be of great importance as an expressive tool in soloing. B.B. King is a master of this technique; he will at times abandon his usual top two- or three-string position and go to the low strings for a little "growl." I love this style because it shows you and the listener that excitement need not be the result of only a treble-string lick. I believe that one of the primary reasons rock and blues players spend most of their time away from the lower strings is that it *feels* uncomfortable. If you're playing something like a Gibson Les Paul, with a fat, wide, and very flat neck, you might be inclined to feel a little shortchanged by the time you get to the *D* string, especially if you have small hands. Of course, a classical guitarist, with hand arched high above the fretboard, would have no problems with these strings, but ask them to properly bend one of the notes, or give it a bluesy vibrato? Forget it. I suppose the answer is in finding the right neck for you, because as rock players, we don't want to compromise the proper techniques we need so much for string bending and the like.

As far as hand positions go, I always say that if the string is intersecting your finger at approximately a 45° angle, you're playing in the proper way for rock techniques. In the photo of a *G* string being slightly bent, you can see the angle I'm referring to.

In the lick in Ex. 20, we see how we can combine the techniques of sliding, hammering on, pulling off, and, of course, phrasing to create a rather explosive style.

A technique usually reserved for the higher strings—that of repetitious hammer-ons—is used to great effect on the *A* and *D* strings in Ex. 21.

Ex. 20

Ex. 21

Leads and Solos 15

Ex. 22

Ex. 23

Ex. 24

In the next position (Ex. 22), one of my all time favorites, the lick is played in a continuous *downward* motion. Note that while we can use three fingers for the pull-off lick on the *G* string, we can use a slide to create the same effect for a lower version of the same lick, on the *A* string.

This string-bending position in Ex. 23 is one of the more difficult ones, because while your whole hand must be committed to the bent note as always, you must bend extra hard and accurately to raise the *D* string a whole-step. Make sure the bend is down, or away from you.

Now let's examine a nice, fat, Hendrix-like position, which I like to use on the lower strings, created by a partial barre in the *D* and *G* strings (Ex. 24). Remember to eliminate the barre as soon as it's no longer needed, to avoid tying up your left hand.

Rock soloing: getting faster

■ Having discussed rock soloing on the lower strings, the next step would seem rather obvious. However, before simply moving on to the higher strings, there are several crucial concepts to consider. One of the most important and desirable attributes for a lead player is the ability to play fast. I believe in this, not so much to create seemingly endless and monotonous repetitions of notes (as can be heard far too often), but to have the ability and speed at your disposal. In other words, when the feeling grabs you, whether it be for a burst of emotion or simply to show off, it would be nice to be able to make your fingers work just as fast as your ideas are coming.

When I started learning guitar, I was completely self-taught, and not being one of the most disciplined kids around, I found that my "practicing" consisted mainly of running through what I *did* know with as much speed as possible. This actually wasn't such a bad way to practice, and what I lacked in fingerboard knowledge I made up for in heart and sheer desire. In any event, rapid picking and a combination of good left-hand techniques, such as hammer-ons and pull-offs, are the path towards becoming a better fast player. Here we'll focus on some specific exercises to develop coordination between rapid-fire picking and left-hand accuracy.

Ex. 25

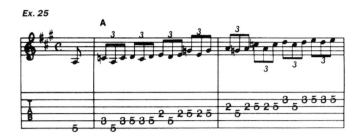

Ex. 26

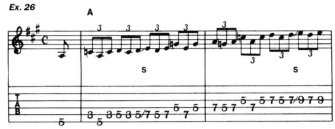

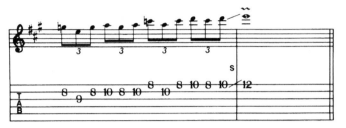

Ex. 27

Ex. 28

Ex. 25 is a familiar fast run that goes from the low *E* string to the high *E*. This should work with the time-honored three-fingered rock approach for the left hand. Therefore, I recommend trying to use your 1st and 3rd fingers for the rather difficult 2nd- to 5th-fret stretches. This exercise should employ an even down-and-up picking approach—in fact, it should really help you develop this technique. Start it slowly at first (with an up-stroke), and *please* don't be discouraged if things don't come so quickly!

In Ex. 26, we're essentially using the same idea as before, except that now, with a few well-placed *slides*, we're able to shift positions and substitute for a picked note. As you'll also notice, we are now extending the position so much that we are *adding* quite a few notes in the process.

In Ex. 27, a very Knopfler-esque little lick, we see how rapid-fire picking and left-hand accuracy can create an exciting effect within very small confines. Note that as the position keeps repeating itself, it becomes almost second nature, like an echo unit repeating over and over, giving the lick a feeling of ambiguity.

The scale shown in Ex. 28 starts with the same position as in the last lick, then works its way down the strings. Accent the first note of each four-note pattern to break the monotony and give a better sense of movement and phrasing.

Keep in mind that these are better played in a three-fingered rock style, but if the stretches are really beyond you, I'm certainly not a pinky-hater.

We've now covered some of the ways to maximize speed on the fingerboard. These are important exercises, and it would do you well to have them under your belt before going on.

Rock soloing: rapid-fire pull-offs

■ I like to think of playing fast as a relative thing. There are players who, when you first hear them, are so fast and so clean that they make you never want to pick up a guitar again. Then there are players who are more impressive with their ability to play melodically and with feeling, and *then* they throw in some very fast runs as part of the *whole*. Many of *these* players are not really as fast as the first type I mentioned, yet their effect is often more appealing. Sure, if you play nothing but flash licks all the time, you'll be fast, but you won't be truly musical—which is what we're really after.

One of the skills rock guitarists must have at their disposal, if they expect to play fast, is proper pull-off technique. We've touched on this before, but it's important to focus on some particular pull-off positions in a rock context. Hammer-ons, which we've also been working on, don't really relate to pull-offs as much as you would think. While a hammer-on is created by coming straight down onto the string with your finger, a pull-off is not, as many think, the exact reverse. Rather than this relatively silent "lift-off" of the note, the pull-off really consists of a left-hand *pluck*. The fretting finger actually plucks the string again after the fretted note is picked—in a downward motion, *away* from you. This requires having the lowest finger anchored firmly so that the string isn't pulled sharp by the left-hand's plucking action.

Ex. 29 is very similar to Ex. 28, only it is played incorporating pull-offs rather than all picked notes. Try to get this one to sound real rapid fire.

Ex. 30 requires a difficult left-hand stretch, particularly if you play it like I do, with the 3rd finger playing the highest note. This run applies to *A* minor, and is great for getting a bluesy feel.

In Ex. 31 we see that by creating a partial barre over two strings, and then releasing the middle note of the last position, we turn our *A* minor lick into a *C* major lick. Again, *try* to make the stretch with your 3rd finger.

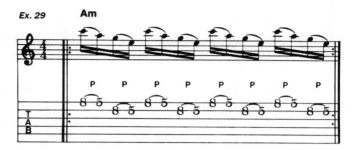

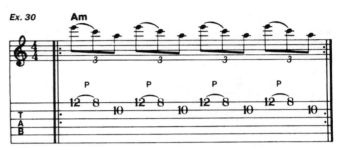

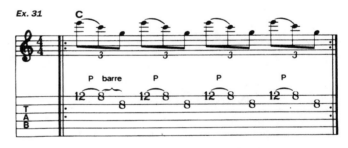

"Hats Off" (Ex. 32) shows how you can imply several chord changes by just the slightest shift of notes within a relatively consistent position. Remember, there are no hammer-ons in this piece, just pull-offs, and you should pluck down, but not so far away as to make the return to the position difficult.

"HATS OFF"

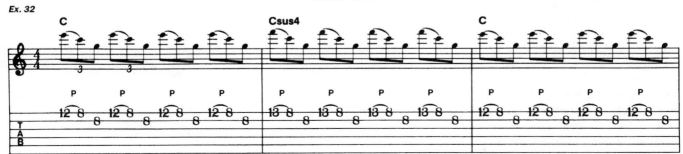

➤

Ex. 32 continued

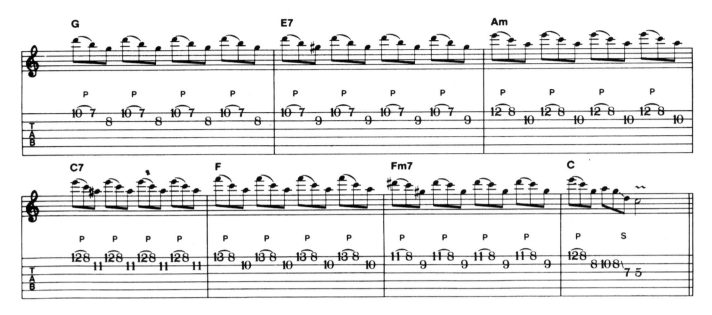

Rock soloing: rapid-fire picking

■ We've been concentrating for some time now on the left hand's job in rock soloing. This is where the eloquence, the expressiveness of the guitar comes from, in my opinion. The right, or picking hand, of course, is the guiding force behind all of this expression. However, when slides, hammer-ons, and pull-offs are emphasized, the right hand never gets a chance to realize its full potential. For this reason, now's a good time to focus on picking and developing a style well suited to rapid-fire playing.

You should hold the pick in the proper way, between the thumb and forefinger, with very little of it showing, and not gripped too tightly or loosely. It should be held just firmly enough so that it moves with some resistance when attacking the strings with force. Many players like to anchor the heel of their picking hand at the bridge, especially when incorporating a lot of left-hand stylistic techniques. This is fine—in fact, I've played this way for years—but when I really want to get serious about my picking speed, I always move my hand up on the strings, away from the bridge, and try to keep the same angle of attack for each and every string. This is so important for

maintaining your picking speed, because if you want to play fast, a consistent attack on each note is crucial.

To get into picking this way, practice Ex. 33 carefully alternating downstrokes and upstrokes. Keep your hand above the strings; with a nice, relaxed wrist, move your hand up one string at a time, maintaining the same angle each time. You should do this in the opposite direction, as well. Play it over and over, and try to pick up speed each time. You'll find that this becomes a good warm-up exercise.

Chromatic runs are always very conducive to rapid picking, and wherever you see possibilities for them within scales, you should try to experiment and find

Ex. 33

➡

some new ones for yourself. I like to use the first three fingers of my left hand for three-note chromatic licks, and often walk them up in groups of three on the same string. Ex. 34 is a good example.

When a passage consists of many whole-step jumps, such as in the classic blues pentatonic scale, chromatic figures can help fill a lot of the gaps and create some really nice fast runs (Ex. 35).

The position in Ex. 36 shows how this style of picking can create some pretty mean licks within very close quarters. This is a blues-based run, and it utilizes the lowered 5th on the *B* string, as opposed to the usual position on the *G* string. To make this move properly, you'll have to drop that index finger down one fret and move it over to the *B* string just in time to make the note. It will then have to return to the *G* string for the last part of the lick.

Remember to start slow and increase the tempo with each pass.

Using dissonance to your advantage

■ Dissonance—or the sounding of notes that harmonically "clash" with either a chord or single notes—is the heart and soul of some of the most tasteful blues, rock, and country licks around. To convey this to the listener, true and proper understanding of these "harmonic outcasts" is a must.

While many licks may include notes dissonant to the relative chord, they really don't take on the true discordant character unless they're overlapping other notes or sustained for a long time. For example, if a guitarist were to hold out a long, bend D# over an A chord, it would create a real cliff-hanging situation, as if the note simply hadn't bent far enough. The ear naturally wants to hear a *resolution* to a proper note from the chord or scale, and this knowledge, put into the hands of a creative musician, can give birth to new ideas, emotionally and musically.

In blues and rock licks, dissonance usually takes the form of lowered 5ths. This is probably the truest "blue note," and has given birth to countless blues melodies over the years. The difference here is that it is usually used as a *passing tone* from the 4th and 5th of the scale and rarely gets this much attention or accentuation within a lick. In the case of the runs below, it's important to maintain fingering the lowered 5ths for as long as you can in relation to the notes that might follow or overlap them. It is this sustain that creates the true clash of notes that we are looking for in the melodic structure. In Ex. 37, we make extensive use of hammer-ons and pull-offs to help create the "blur" effect that the dissonant notes should have.

The licks in Ex. 38 come from the lowered 5th position that lies on the *G* string—again, creating a dissonance with the overlapping perfect 5th on the *B* string.

→

If we move these down a step-and-a-half (three frets), we see how they become dissonant country runs when juxtaposed against the same chord. In Ex. 39, the dissonant notes take on the role of lowered *3rds*, as opposed to the previous lowered *5ths*.

Open positions are very useful for dissonant runs, as well, and lend themselves to some pretty outrageous-sounding licks. In Ex. 40, we see a similar group of runs, except that now they have the convenience of the added open-string notes.

For the major pentatonic, country type of dissonant lick with the major 3rd, open *G* offers the best possibilities for using open strings. Here are a few choices in Ex. 41, but you should try to make up some of your own, in all of the positions I've illustrated.

Using dissonance within major positions

■ Lowered fifths and lowered thirds as *dissonant* notes are only the tip of the iceberg. Just about *any* notes can become dissonant, depending simply on how far out you're taking the harmonic center of the dissonance.

Once again, I'd like to emphasize the technique of using both pick and fingers together to get that nice, even "roll" that's so useful in these positions. You *can* use a

pick alone, of course, and if you're really smooth with it, I'm sure you'll have no problems getting the licks to sound right.

In any event, I like to use this technique for melodic runs that include open-string notes. The run in Ex. 42, which is actually the *E* major scale, uses some pretty tricky timing of the open-string notes and lateral move-

➤

ment of the fretted notes. I use it as an introduction to my song "North Sea" on my album *Hot Pickups* [Rounder].

In the next position in Ex. 43, we're merely changing a few choice notes to turn it into a *minor* scale run that resolves nicely into the *E* chord at the end.

Open *G* also has some nice melodic usages of the major scale dissonances, and in next two examples we see a run that starts with two *G*'s together, on the *D* and *G* strings, in a position that lends itself perfectly to a dissonant descending run. Here, it is written in two ways: first, in Ex. 44, we see how it can be played in block chord form, using either fingerpicking or flatpicking and fingers to get the even, solid attack; next, in Ex. 45, is the same position, only broken up into three-note rolls. This creates a very effective, almost banjo-like sound on the guitar.

Though in the same open area, Ex. 46 uses the descending major lick an octave higher. This time, the dissonance is created by the open *G* string played against the descending notes on the higher string.

Hammer-ons that create more than one extra note on a given string can help give a smooth, linear approach in some of these major-scale dissonances. In Ex. 47 we are *ascending* in the open *E* position of the major scale, on both the *B* and *E* strings, and then using pull-offs to reverse the situation. Let the dissonant notes ring as long as possible to overlap with the other notes.

If we start experimenting with combining positions, we see how the major scale *and* blues scale dissonances can work together for some interesting possibilities (Ex. 48).

The possibilities are endless. The discoveries just start to unfold the more you experiment, improvise, and set challenges and goals for yourself.

Ex. 44

Ex. 45

Ex. 46

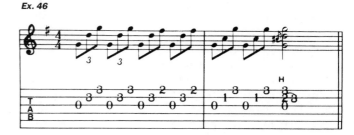

Ex. 47

Ex. 48

Ex. 42

Ex. 43

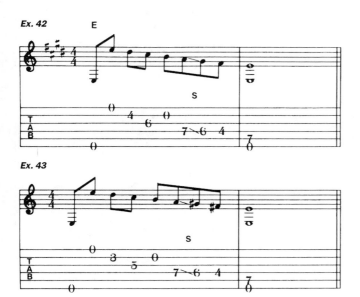

Building your solos

■ When I give clinics, it seems inevitable that someone in the audience comes up with the impossible question of all time, "How do you construct your solos?" Another favorite is, "What do you think about when you're soloing?" Well, of couse, the answer to the latter is: "Nothing!" And the former's answer, in its truest form, of course, is simply, "I don't know; I just do it." This is all true, as many of you self-taught players out there understand. It's almost impossible to put into words what comes out of you as a result of the strictly primitive drive to create, because you are truly speaking through your instrument. However, there are ways of analyzing what does go into the makeup of a given solo or soloing approach, particularly if you're able to step back and take a look at yourself or someone else objectively.

To a certain degree, many of us build our solos on the statement-and-answer first established by early blues styles. Since we are dealing with notes and not words, what we are saying is far more abstract, so our means of getting there are far more flexible than something as limiting as lyrics. Once you start a solo, that first statement made on the guitar must set the tone for everything else that follows. Your solo itself must exist in time and space as a whole, just like a painting, a song, or any other work of art. From first note to last, you are making a statement of how you see the song and how you see your solo as part of that song. Certainly one of today's biggest problems is that too many people think a solo must follow the same predictable pattern, and the solo becomes more of a bag of tricks rather than something that has some meaning.

Anyway, enough of this preaching, and on with some music. Space doesn't permit me to write out a long solo for you here, but that doesn't really matter: a great statement can be made in a very short time, as well. In fact, that's actually preferable more often than not. In the solo in Ex. 49, notice the careful attention to overall balance. Though the chords are not typical in the blues sense, the question-and-answer approach is still very much prevalent. Also note the importance of varying your speed during the solo. You must let some parts of the solo "breathe," while other parts must express emotional outbursts with more concentrated flurries of notes.

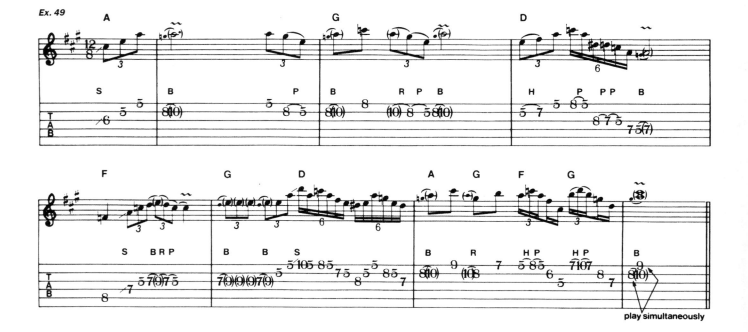

Ex. 49

play simultaneously

Slide Licks

Using slides to move around the neck

■ Left-hand sliding is one of the lead guitarist's major tools, but is rarely used for more than an obligatory slide into a note. I feel that this technique is as vocal and interesting as string bending, hammering on, or pulling off, and deserves to be examined more closely.

One of the first ways of seeing just how flexible these slides are is to view them in the context of scales. Slides are among the main ways the left hand can move smoothly from one position to another without having to pick another note, and with sliding you can shift around the neck quite a bit. Ex. 1 is one blues scale that uses two slides between the same notes at three different positions. In this case, we're always sliding between the fourth and the fifth of the scale.

The major pentatonic scale in *C* uses a very similar position, except that now the notes that are slid become the second and the major third of the scale (Ex. 2).

In Ex. 3, this version of the major pentatonic scale utilizes even more of the neck, and therefore more slides, as well. The next-to-last slide should be played with the 2nd finger, as opposed to the 3rd.

With the use of these slides and some very carefully placed hammer/pull licks, we can really make these scales into some interesting and rather complex runs (Ex. 4). Note how these back up one string at a time, creating neat little groups of two-string licks. Execute the hammer-on part of the lick with the same finger that just played the slide before it.

The major pentatonic offers some great possibilities with this style and makes for a nice connection of two-string patterns. Ex. 5 shows this lick in the key of *G*.

Be sure to practice these scales before we go on. You'll find that they will flow pretty easily once you've played them enough.

Ex. 1

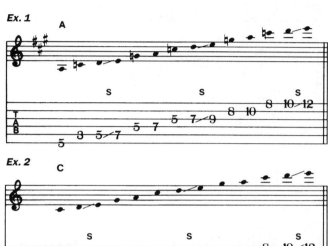

Ex. 2

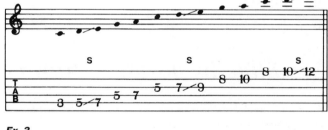

Ex. 3

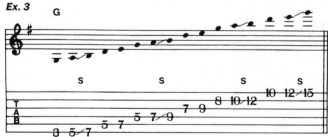

→

Slide in standard tuning

■ When I do clinics, slide guitar is one of my favorite topics. The question of standard tuning versus open tunings comes up quite often. My experience is that standard tuning is more limited than open tunings, which facilitate many marvelous things.

But playing slide in standard tuning does have its advantages, so it's well worth exploring. One very important point is that when you're in standard tuning, your right-hand blocking and damping must be flawless, or else you'll end up with an incredible mess and hit discordant extraneous notes. For this reason, it is imperative that you *fingerpick*, which enables you to block and damp with more accuracy.

The first two photos illustrate the positions I recommend for slide fingerpicking technique and pick/fingers technique. Observe how the fingers are poised to play, and how the thumb damps the strings.

The third photo shows the proper position of the slide. Notice how the fingers lightly drag behind the slide, damping extraneous sounds, and that the slide is long enough so that the tip of the pinky can sense the end of the slide, which enables you to play single-notes on the lower strings with more accuracy.

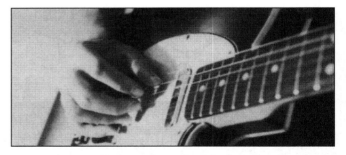

Ex. 6 shows a blues pentatonic scale fingering designed for slide; it requires that you make full use of your damping abilities. Only when you reach the 9th fret do you have the luxury of a three-note chord to fall back on. On the other hand open *E* tuning [*E, B, E, G#, B, E,* low to high], provides *many* possibilities for chordal playing.

The licks in Ex. 7 are from a "box" pattern based around the *E* chord at the 9th fret, which contains a wealth of possibilities.

Based on this same "box" pattern, this group of ideas strays from the position a bit more, requiring more sophisticated damping (Ex. 8). When you take the slide up to the 12th fret, for example, it's very important to lay your right-hand thumb across the bottom strings, in order to prevent unwanted notes.

Ex. 6

Ex. 7

Ex. 8

More standard-tuning slide

Let's look at standard-tuning slide playing in the context of actual soloing. I think it's really important to approach slide playing chordally, whenever possible. In standard tuning, the major chord form occurs on the *D, G,* and *B* strings. (This is the same triad that you find in the open-position *A* and *G* chords.) This voicing occurs occasionally in the solo. It helps to break up the single-note lines and it clarifies the chord changes.

I wholeheartedly recommend using fingerpicking technique to play the solo because right-hand damping is

essential in creating a clean sound and style. Also, please be careful to use only as much slide as is necessary for a given position. For example, when you play the triad on the *D, G,* and *B* strings, try not to let the slide extend beyond the *D* string. Lightly dragging your left-hand fingers behind the slide helps to damp out any unwanted notes on the low *E* and *A* strings.

So here we have it! (See. Ex. 9.) Take it slowly at first and, above all, concentrate on getting as *clean* a sound as possible.

Ex. 9

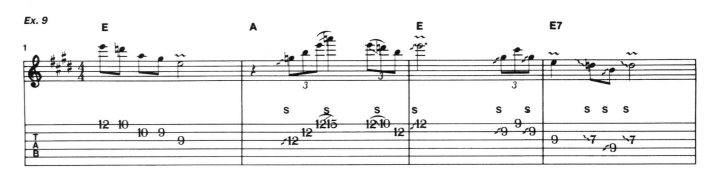

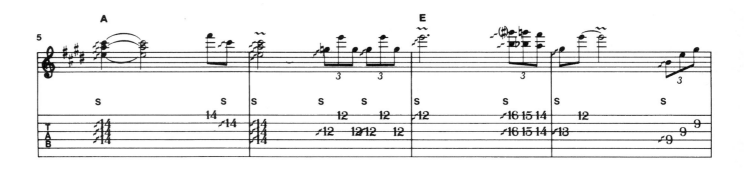

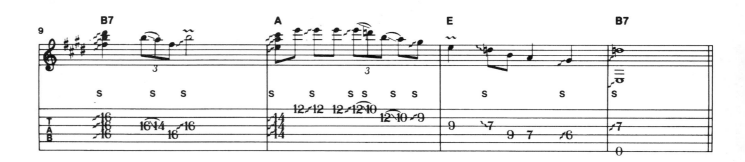

Slide for sissies

■ Well, okay, not really. I mean, calling standard-tuning slide "slide for sissies" is like calling a capo a "cheater," which of course, it isn't. In the right hands, it's actually a very creative tool, and both are techniques that enable you to do things that a normal guitar situation wouldn't allow. The "sissy" part is based on the fact that many people start playing standard-tuning slide without realizing that the sounds they are trying to emulate were created in open tunings by traditional slide players such as Elmore James, Robert Johnson, Tampa Red, and others. Some guitarists even try to play the sounds with a pick, which makes it *twice* as sissy, because fingerpicking is really the best way to go for any kind of slide work—damping and muting become so much more difficult without it.

When I shot a Hot Licks video with former Rolling Stone Mick Taylor, I was astounded by what a clean sound he got playing slide with a pick and in standard tuning. The only problem is that this method creates a sound closer to regular fretted notes than anything else, due to the extreme damping required, which makes

things sound rather staccato. Nevertheless, slide is an important technique for all guitarists to have in their arsenals, and this lesson is for those of you who don't fool with fingerpicking or open tunings.

Standard-tuning slide has far fewer harmony-note possibilities than, say, open-*E* tuning. In open tunings, your chord positions reach across all six strings, but in standard tuning, the only available major chord occurs across the *D, G*, and *B* strings. It's around this position that the "box" pattern lies, with the most opportunities for lead improvising. In the key of *E*, for example, this is at the 9th fret, while in open-*E* tuning it involves all the strings at the 12th fret. To play, in standard tuning, the blues scale that starts at the 12th fret on the high *E* string and ends at the 12th fret on the low *E* string in open-*E* tuning, one has to travel from the same starting point all the way to the 7th fret on the *A* string! If you don't damp at all, the open-tuning version at least sounds like an *E* chord, while the standard-tuning version sounds like a blur of dissonance.

You should hold the slide on your little finger, and try to get a slide that allows your finger *just* enough exposure at the end so you can "sense" the end of the slide (and, therefore, the string you're playing). It's also important to keep the slide angle perpendicular to the strings, and to only cover the strings that are necessary. This helps damping quite a bit and eliminates a lot of unwanted noise. Ex. 10 shows some of my favorite standard-tuning slide licks. Hope you enjoy!

Ex. 10

Ex. 10 continued

Even more standard-tuning slide

■ Okay, okay. So standard-tuning slide is not "slide for sissies"—it's slide for wimps! Just kidding—in fact, I've been kidding all along. It's just not *traditional* slide playing, and therefore relates only remotely to the sounds of Delta blues, Chicago blues, or even country slide.

But there are certain licks and positions that are common to both standard tuning and the more versatile open tunings. Keep in mind that proper blocking and damping are essential in order to get a clean sound in standard-tuning slide, because we don't have all those nice chords and harmonies to fall back on, as we do in open tuning. Of course, the big advantage to standard-tuning slide is that it can become just one element in your bag of tricks, and you can throw it into your style without having to change your tuning.

I like using open-position licks for slide guitar, and standard tuning is no exception. A few nice harmony positions do exist in standard tuning, but when it comes to playing standard-sounding blues licks, you'll have to follow the notes as you do when playing regular lead guitar, using some very critical and deft left- and right-hand damping. The examples illustrate just what I'm talking about. Ex. 11 to 14 use open-string notes as melody notes

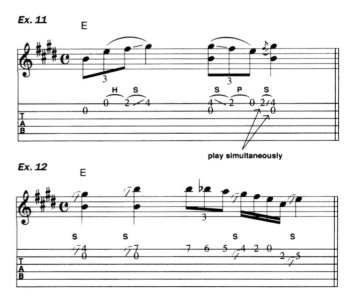

Ex. 11

play simultaneously

Ex. 12

or harmonies, while Ex. 15 to 17 are very much like "closed"-position blues licks, but played with a slide rather than your fingers. Ex. 15 and Ex. 16 illustrate the difficulty of using standard-tuning slide to simulate regular lead playing. Have fun, and be sure to experiment as much as possible with this challenging style.

Ex. 13 G

Ex. 14 G

Ex. 15 A

Ex. 16 A

Ex. 17 A

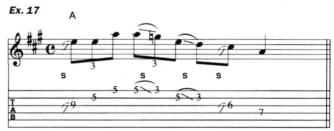

Fake slide

■ Even if you don't play slide, you can incorporate some cool, cryin' slide-like sounds into your style. By artfully mixing string bends, finger slides, and vibrato you can emulate—okay, *fake*—slide without wearing a Coricidin bottle on your pinkie.

When faking slide, it's important to downplay the more percussive techniques—hammer-ons, trills, tapping, and so on. Shoot for an uncluttered, sustained sound. Try to avoid typical fingerings; use slides and con-

nected bends whenever possible. Prebends, which you slowly release to your target note, are also really effective. These techniques are featured in Ex. 18 to 22. Additionally, Ex. 21 and 22 illustrate how you can use open strings in conjunction with your fingered notes the way a slide player does.

If you have a whammy bar, try incorporating dips and rises into your licks to further enhance the slip-slidin' effect. Keep experimenting!

→

Ex. 18

Ex. 19

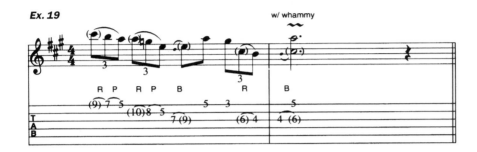

Ex. 20

Ex. 21

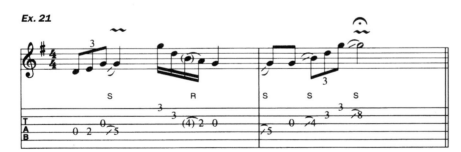

Ex. 22

Hot Rhythm Guitar

Smokin' R&B rhythms

■ So far we have focused on the "hotter" aspects of lead guitar playing. Now let's turn to the subject of hot rhythm guitar.

Rhythm guitar, though a separate entity unto itself, should always be thought of as an integral aspect of lead guitar playing. A part is a part, and should be approached as such if you expect to be well-rounded as a guitarist. Rhythm guitar is a true art form, and can contain as much restraint and release as some of the most complex soloing imaginable. Much of the rhythm playing required by a guitarist in a band situation takes the form of partial chords, rather than full 6-string chords. The optimum conditions arise when the picking hand is allowed to move freely, with the fretting hand having to do a fair degree of blocking and damping, "squeezing" the notes of the chord only when you wish them to be heard. This enables you to continue to feel the groove, while not sacrificing clean playing. This is the type of playing heard in early R&B and later funk styles, best exemplified by players such as Steve Cropper, Cornell Dupree, Curtis Mayfield, and Niles Rodgers.

When laying down a rhythm part, I like to think of my right hand as playing two parts of the drum kit—the high hat and the snare. The high hat is the more constant "time," usually played on the lower, bassy strings, while the snare's backbeat is whacked across the brighter-sounding top strings. To illustrate just what on earth I'm talking about, try this rhythmic exercise (Ex. 1): damp out all the strings with your left hand, so only a percussive sound is heard. Then, using alternate up- and down-strokes, play the pattern as illustrated in the following tablature. Note the use of low strings for the most part, while the high strings are whacked for the *backbeats*.

Now, using the left-hand damping with a combination of note squeezing, try the rhythm part in Ex. 2, directly based on the pattern we just learned.

Perhaps the most rewarding use of this rhythm technique is when you can actually juxtapose a seemingly independent guitar part against the percussive right-hand "drum" part. This obviously requires a great deal of concentration to get the proper separation between right- and left-hand duties to make them work in perfect coordination with each other. It takes some hard practice, but the results are worth it, and people watching and listening will be amazed at the sounds you're able to create.

The true secret lies in that chord squeezing I've been talking about. This enables your left hand to let the notes ring only when *you* want them to, regardless of pick direction or musical dynamics. This will create that independent "guitar and drum" sound.

Ex. 1

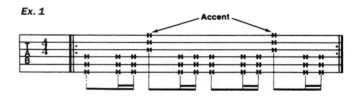

Ex. 2

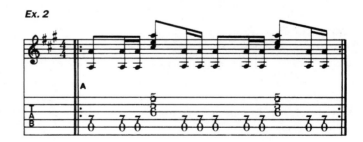

In Ex. 3, a favorite rockabilly/gospel lick of mine, you can see how the musical pattern breaks up the unrelenting pulse of the right-hand—which, by the way, is *still* the one we've been using. Start the lick with your fingers in the form of the partial *A7* chord, only don't press down. Play it as the damped "drum" part first. Then, when you feel ready, introduce the chords to the pattern. The quick *D* chord is created by a partial barre using the ring finger, while the *A7* is based on a partial barre played by the index finger. If it doesn't work out at first, go back to the "drum" figure and try, try again. Like I said, this one may take some time doing before it feels right, but when it does, *watch out!*

Ex. 3

Combining rhythm work with single notes

■ The last lesson introduced the concept of just how important the right hand's silent (as well as audible) work is to truly rhythmic R&B guitar. Well, there are a lot of things that the right hand can actually be *playing* instead of all the damped-out percussive work we encountered in the last lesson. Mind you, it's still an essential style, and something I hope you can master—especially since it illustrates a true understanding of what you are doing in a rhythmic sense: becoming a part of the group's sound and groove. When combining single-note work with rhythm guitar, however, we are striving to create that same rhythmic drive while filling in all the spaces with notes, effectively creating *two* distinct yet interwoven parts.

As in last month's lesson, be sure to keep your picking hand free and loose, because the act of going from lead notes to rhythm parts should *not* constitute any noticeable added tension in your picking hand. It just reflects a different type of accuracy, combined with a subtle use of left-hand damping.

For instance, in Ex. 4 we are creating a very definite eighth-note feel while combining "lead-up" bass notes (what bassists might call a walking bass line, leading into the rhythm chords) with a very Steve Cropper-like rhythm part. We are using the *C7* position of *E7*; note how this enables us to make use of open *E* at certain opportune times.

Ex. 4 E7

Ex. 5 E7

Ex. 6 E9

Ex. 5 is a variation on our first lick, this time with a more rapid-fire approach to the bass line. Try getting to a point where you can play it rather briskly. Using 9th chords in this style is very prevalent in R&B music, one example of this being saxophonist King Curtis' records (featuring Cornell Dupree on guitar). For this chord position I recommend using your 3rd finger for the *E* on the *A* string, the middle finger for the *G#* on the *D* string, and your pinky for the three-string barre at the top of the chord. I know this is probably *not* the way you ordinarily play this chord (something I never understood, since this position *is* an outgrowth of the normal *C* position), but it will eventually become clear that it helps the combining of chromatic bass lead-ups and rhythm fills. Examples 6 and 7 illustrate how you can use the 9th chord position to alter the sound of the previous two examples.

If you want to really get flashy, a more funky style would be in order for the rhythm fill. Imagine a full-fledged horn section wailing and doing steps to the lick in Ex. 8, and then you'll be on the right track.

Remember to keep that right hand nice and loose, and play it funky.

Double-stops in R&B guitar

■ R&B music does not live by funkiness alone, and the slower ballad forms have given birth to some of the sweetest guitar styles around—styles that have an even subtler use of melody and dynamics, and are just as much a trademark of R&B guitar as the well-known flashier licks. At the root of many of these sweeter sounds is the use of double-stops, or two-note positions. Much of this playing is done in the major pentatonic mode, giving it a more "optimistic" sound that is well-served in the sweet soul ballads in which we've come to expect these licks. Guitarists such as Curtis Mayfield, Bobby Womack, Cornell Dupree, Steve Cropper, and Jimmy Johnson (of the Muscle Shoals Rhythm Section) come to mind when I play or think about this style, and it would be wise to check out some of the great records they have played on—with people like Sam Cooke, Otis Redding, Percy Sledge, King Curtis, and Arthur Conley—to better understand the genre.

When listening to these recordings and other soul ballads, you will notice that double-stop licks are used primarily as fills behind the vocal and between lines, as opposed to being used in a soloing situation. This is not because they're inappropriate for solos; quite the contrary, it's just that stylistically, R&B soul music rarely has guitar solos. When it does, the approach is usually a bit more hard-hitting. *Never* feel confined to only the way in which a technique is demonstrated; if no one experimented in this way, music itself would come to a near standstill.

In this double-note style, R&B probably bears more resemblance to country than to blues, especially when you throw in the fact that we're playing in the country-oriented major pentatonic mode. The use of hammer-ons and pull-offs combined with stationary harmony notes is probably the most country-flavored approach in R&B guitar playing. In fact, the more you study the two styles, the clearer the similarities become, particularly when the sound is gospel-oriented.

➜

Ex. 9 illustrates the use of a quick hammer-on and pull-off combined with the stationary note. In actuality, the hammer-on is creating a quick IV chord by adding its major 3rd, but the pull-off happens too quickly to make it sound like any more than a grace note. Remember that the pull-off is really a *left-hand pluck;* therefore, the note is actually created by the downward plucking motion of the finger—in this case, the 3rd finger.

In Ex. 10, almost the same position is achieved, only now we use the sweet, soulful sound of double-note *slides* to create a sound familiar to so many R&B tunes. The opening slide—temporarily adding a 6th and 9th to the lick—uses the index finger as a partial barre. The second position is played with the 3rd finger on the *B* string and the 2nd finger on the *G* string. Note how it ends up in a sort of unresolved voicing that you may recognize from various records.

Of course, as is the case with almost anything on the guitar, a lick can be played in another position, another octave, or both. This double-note pentatonic scale (Ex.11) is evidence of some of the more accessible places where this double-stop style can be practiced. In fact, the exercise is a pretty nice lick in itself, and with some hammer-ons and pull-offs thrown in can sound almost like two guitarists playing in harmony! I will explore this more in the next chapter, but for now I'd like you to experiment on your own.

If you're currently doing a back-up gig where there isn't a lot of room for riffing, you may want to try subtly throwing in some of these double-stops (with care of placement, of course). You might be pleasantly surprised with the results, and so will the person you're accompanying. In any event, I hope you can put this style to good use in whatever you're doing.

Ex. 9

Ex. 10

Ex. 11

Hot Memphis rhythm

■ Let's explore the Memphis-style R&B rhythms made so popular by players such as Steve Cropper and Cornell Dupree. The most identifiable part of this style is its combination of funky rhythms with occasional two- or three-note fills thrown in for some spice. This dual demand upon the right hand requires a good, loose, playing approach, as well as a neat left-hand damping technique. Many of the licks often involve either a one-finger slide of a two- or three-note chord, or a bend. We'll deal with both of these in this lesson.

First, let's just concentrate on the licks themselves (Ex. 12), so you can get a clear idea of just the sound you

want to get across. This also gives you a chance to practice the necessary damping, so play them as if they're part of the overall rhythm, with a strong right hand approach over all the strings.

Assuming you've got that fairly well down we can now combine the lead and rhythm together. Remember that the bulk of the playing consists of the rhythm part, and that the lead work acts mainly as punctuation, or accents to the overall rhythm pattern. You'll note that in Ex. 13, we make use of both types of fills: the two-note licks with bends, and the chordal slides. Remember to keep it funky and smooth at the same time. Have fun!

R&B rhythm guitar

■Rhythm guitar is becoming a lost art form. My favorite rhythm guitar style is that of great R&B players like Bobby Womack (with Sam Cooke), Cornell Dupree, Steve Cropper, and Curtis Mayfield—all heavily influenced by gospel playing. The sparse instrumentation of gospel music lends itself to this sweet type of guitar playing, which combines sensitive rhythm work with delicate lead fills. Double-note runs and country-style hammer-ons are common, too.

Arpeggios are another important part of this style. They give the playing a soulful feel, and they work really well with the little lead fills you can throw in now and then. You can also break up the monotony of the steady arpeggios with appropriate punctuation like hammer-ons, pull-offs, and slides.

To hear the true essence of the style I'm trying to capture here, listen to tunes like Sam Cooke's "Bring It On Home To Me" or Otis Redding's "I've Been Loving You Too Long." The example (Ex.14) is a soul ballad-type rhythm guitar part that utilizes many of the techniques I've mentioned. Try it at a moderate tempo, almost as if you were supporting a vocal. Play with a lot of soul—that's much more important than getting the notes exactly right.

Ex. 14

Double-Stops

Chuck Berry's double-stop flash

■ Chuck Berry is, to me, the father of rock and roll guitar. It was he who took his blues roots along with the true feeling of the 1950s and created a sound and style all his own. His incredibly hard-driving guitar style, along with lyrics that possessed the most vivid rock and roll imagery of all time, helped permanently shape the future of rock and R&B.

When one thinks of Chuck Berry's guitar style, two major elements come to mind: (1) his well-known shuffles (without which, even heavy metal might not exist); and (2) the flashy, trademark licks he'd use to introduce his songs. "Roll Over Beethoven," "Carol," "Johnny B. Goode," and "Sweet Little Sixteen" are just a few of the classics that begin with Chuck's much-imitated intro licks.

Chuck Berry is a master at playing double-stops, or two-note licks, and this is certainly one of *the* most recognizable elements of his style. Most guitarists require two fingers for this task; however, upon seeing Chuck perform on numerous occasions, it's pretty clear to me that, for the most part, he manages to play these positions with *one* finger—due to the fact that he has simply *enormous* hands and fingers! In fact, Berry plays a first-position *E* chord with only two fingers: his 2nd finger frets both the *A* and *D* strings, while his index frets the *G* string.

As you'll no doubt see in Ex. 1 to 3, this double-stop technique requires a great deal of *partial barring* on the part of the index finger—usually depressing either the top two strings or the *B* and *G* strings. In Ex. 1, we see the necessity for accuracy on the part of the left hand by combining elements of sliding, single notes, and partial barring.

In Ex. 2, you must start in the barre position, and then quickly shift to the two-fingered two-note style, as the index finger shifts its barre over one more string to accommodate the hammer-on.

Finally, Ex. 3 shows an example of a full-fledged Chuck Berry intro, where we put all of the elements together.

Note how the double-note slides add to the power of the accents. Remember to keep that index finger moving its barre along, and to get it out of the way when you need to do the single-note work at the end of the intro. Have fun with it, and don't forget that rubber leg, boy!

Ex. 1

Ex. 2

Ex. 3

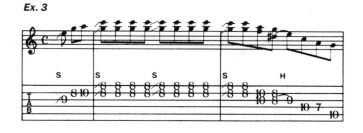

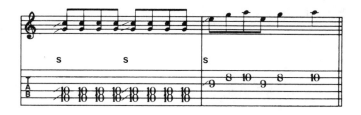

Making two-note patterns from chord positions

■ Let's discuss one of the many little tricks that can spice up your playing: creating double-note runs from chord positions. I often feel like throwing some harmony licks into an already established single-note solo, while not wanting to stray too far from the position I'm already in. When I first began experimenting with this style, I found that it was really easy for me to find new positions, and that the licks quickly became part of my repertoire.

One key is that while these licks *do* involve chord positions, you rarely have to press down the entire chord all at once, and at times it's easier to use only two notes at a time. This, however, usually occurs when another technique such as sliding or bending is involved, allowing more freedom for the hand to do the technique required.

This first double-note passage (Ex. 4) is from my song, "Paint Job," from the album of the same name [Breaking Records]. It's from the middle bridge section, and I use the double-stops to accentuate the Reggae-Latin type of feel in that part of the song. Note that the chord positions are partial, and the *C* and *D* chords in the first part should use an index-finger barre. Try to play it slightly damped by the heel of your hand, in order to get that Latin steel drum-like effect.

Ex. 5 uses double-note *slides*. In this case, you should have the entire chord ready to be played, but it's only important to press down the two notes needed at any given time. In the first chord position, this isn't very difficult, because we are fretting each note separately. In the 9th chords, however, we are using a barre for the top three notes, so we must train our barre finger to exert the pressure only when it's needed, even though it's covering three strings. Try practicing this piece slowly at first, speeding it up as your confidence grows. You may also want to experiment with a pick-and-fingers style for these licks, enabling the notes to be plucked quite a bit more accurately.

If you're feeling adventurous, put *extensions* (notes beyond those already found in the chord) on top of these chord runs, using your pinky (Ex. 6). In this manner, we're able to extend the sound and the arpeggiation of the chord while reducing the gimmicky sound that sometimes can occur with these kinds of licks. I hope you enjoy them and that these ideas can find their way into your bag of tricks.

Ex. 6

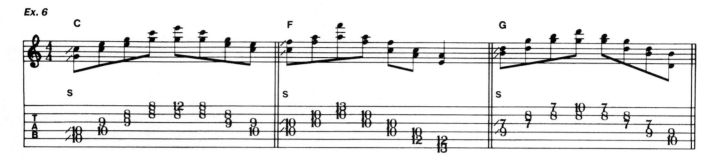

Moving from chord to chord with double-stops

■ Many's the time I've encountered a student who has great fingerboard knowledge but gets "frozen" in his tracks when trying to move from one chord to another with double-note runs. This is truly a common problem and is due in many ways to the ambiguity and sameness of appearance in these types of positions. it's also particularly hard to know what's happening harmonically—the positions not only look alike, but they sound alike, too, and the fact that many are often separated by a string or two further clouds the picture.

One of the fundamental ideas to keep in mind is that we are playing *harmonies* here, and that one note is usually more prominent melodically than the other. This is crucial to your ability to "hear" and predict where some of these patterns are going, especially when improvising and experimenting with them. In your experimentation, you'll find that some patterns are "locked-in" to a chord, while others tend to be more "opened-up" and lend themselves to chord movement.

Some of the more common positions involve the root and the major 3rd of the chord, and can be connected very easily by positions of a similar nature. The simple pattern from *E* to *D* to *A* (Ex. 7) illustrates what I mean. (In these examples, I didn't indicate key signatures, because these chord progressions can be used in many keys.) The first two double-stops should be played with the 1st and 2nd fingers, while those played on the same fret use the *3rd* finger for the high *E* string while the 2nd finger remains "on track" for the *G* string.

With the simple adjustment of just a couple of notes, this same position can be transformed into a pattern that strictly conforms to the *E7* chord (Ex. 8).

Ex. 7

Ex. 8

The fingering pattern in Ex. 9 follows, as we walk it all the way down to the open position.

If you're already in a lower position, such as the *A* position in Ex. 10, you will have to introduce another pair of strings to keep the same idea flowing. In this case, we add the *D* and *B* strings when we run out of room on the *G* and *E*.

The next pattern in Ex. 11, also involving a jump to the *D* and *B* strings, goes directly from *A* to *E*.

Accidents will sometimes happen, and Ex. 12 is the kind of lick that might end up being a trial-and-error "discovery." As you can see, the most subtle shifts can result in some rather startling and intriguing changes.

Please experiment on your own with positions such as these, but be sure to use your fingerboard knowledge and ear to listen for the connections you're making.

Ex. 9

Ex. 10

Ex. 11

Ex. 12

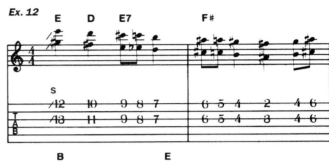

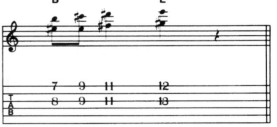

R&B double-stop fills

■ One of the *coolest* guitar sounds around is when you can throw a little lead work in with your rhythm. This occurs particularly often in R&B and funk playing, but it is certainly applicable to other musical styles, as well. At the heart of this sound is the ability to play double-stops, or two-note runs, cleanly and within the rhythmic context you've already laid down as part of the groove. In this way, the overall picture of what you're playing becomes a true *part*, and usually (if you can really lock into a steady pattern with the other musicians) the fills can become as important an element as your chordal work.

→

Ex. 13

Ex. 14

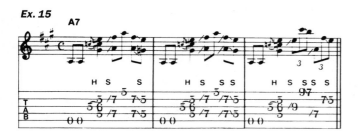

Ex. 15

Ex. 16

The right hand really plays the most important role here, for it's the pattern *it* sets up that determines just what you'll be able to do with the fills. The vocabulary of what you do with the double-stops can be limited, to create some patterns that you can play in your sleep as you drive away at your rhythm licks. The split-string two-note style is very effective and useful here, as the damping that it requires makes it fall right into the percussive sound of damped chords. When I think of this style, the great R&B players such as Jimmy Nolen, Steve Cropper, and Cornell Dupree come to mind; I recommend you pick up some of their recordings to absorb this important approach.

This pattern in Ex. 13 shows how, even within a simple open-position groove, we can do some interesting lead work. Be sure to use your 2nd and 3rd fingers to fret the first two-note lick on the last beat of bar 1, using your index finger to lightly touch and damp out the *B* string. This will enable you to keep your strum across the top three strings relatively percussive and strong.

When we move the *E7* position higher up the neck, we find more double-stops that can also be transferred to adjacent strings when you're feeling adventurous (Ex. 14).

There is a particularly funky lick that works well coming out of a partial chord position, such as Ex. 15. This lick has a high *E*-string note thrown in. It resembles the famed Chuck Berry "Memphis, Tennessee" lick.

You can extend these patterns, provided that you're "locked in" well enough to the groove so that your inventiveness doesn't lead you astray. In Ex. 16, we see how we can mix up both slides and quick strums to create some interesting rhythmic patterns. Remember, keep that downbeat in your sights as you experiment with this kind of pattern, or all hope is lost!

I can't emphasize enough the importance of the right hand in this style, and it's crucial that your left-hand damping be natural and relaxed. Learn to "squeeze" the chords and licks at the right time while you think of your playing in much the way that a drummer would approach it. Try playing nothing but damped patterns for a while—just *chinka-chinks*—and then experiment by throwing in some of the double-stop patterns we've been working on. Find those rhythmic figures that suit you best, and lock into them!

Double-stops with pick & fingers

■ Occasionally I enjoy throwing double-stop licks into the midst of what would normally be a single-note solo. It changes things just enough to be different, and it makes the listener take notice because it's quite obvious, even to the uneducated ear, that a change has taken place.

These double-stops are usually separated by at least one string and employ a combination of pick and finger. In essence, we hold the pick between the forefinger and thumb, and then most of these licks involve the ring finger for the fingerpicked part. Double-stops on adjacent strings involve the pick and middle finger. Remember, when getting ready to play one of these runs, you should have the pick and ring finger in the "ready" position, resting on and ready to play the two strings about to be used. This will increase your accuracy, as well as help damp-out any unwanted tones you might encounter as you get ready to play.

Ex. 17 and 18 have a decidedly bluesy sound to them, and are really substitutes for their single-note counterparts. Take special note of the slides used in the first one.

The runs in Ex. 19 and 20 are also bluesy in nature, but use a contrary motion to get their point across. For those of you who don't know what I'm talking about, a contrary-motion lick consists of one group of notes moving down (often chromatically) while the other group of notes moves up. You'll notice that the second lick of this pair uses a two-string jump instead of a one-string.

The final two runs (Ex. 21 and 22) utilize less two-string movement but are definitely more hammer-on and pull-off oriented. For those of you used to these styles, these runs present the new challenge of letting one finger do the hammers and pulls independently of the other finger, which must hold down its note. Have fun with them—experiment!

Ex. 17

Ex. 18

Ex. 19

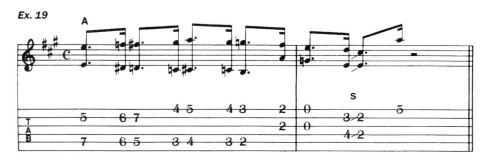

Ex. 20

Ex. 21

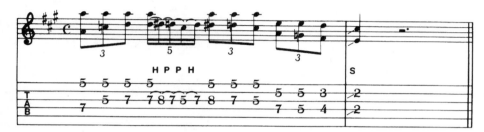

Ex. 22

Using double-stops in blues & country

■ Blues and country styles really lend themselves to double-stop experimentation, and double-stops sound especially exciting when they are occasionally thrown into the middle of a single-note passage. They also communicate to the listener your keen awareness of the inner workings of fretboard harmony—at the drop of a hat, you can harmonize what once would have been a single-note run. The recognizable becomes different and more exciting.

I look at double-stops in two ways: as two-note arpeggiations of a chord, or as moveable harmonized single-note licks. At first, the arpeggio chord forms will be easier to find, especially since you know that the notes will harmonize with each other, no matter what. So let's start with some double-stops in the form of arpeggiated chords. Try using the pick-and-finger approach for Ex. 23, 24, and 25; it provides better blocking, damping, and control.

➡

Ex. 23

play simultaneously

Ex. 24

Ex. 25

Ex. 26, 27, and 28 are more experimental—they utilize the harmonized single-note idea. The pick-and-finger method works especially well for these, as many of the notes are on non-adjacent strings.

Please experiment with this technique—I think you'll be surprised by how much different-sounding stuff you come up with!

Ex. 26

Ex. 27

Ex. 28

Double your twang

■ I like to take an occasional solo consisting only of dual-string licks. When you force yourself to think this way, you're apt to come up with some new ideas and make a unique musical statement. Rockabilly and country players such as Albert Lee and James Burton use double-stops heavily. Rock pioneers Chuck Berry and Eddie Cochran did too.

Ex. 29 to 34 use double-stops to shift positions. This helps you get around the fretboard and open up some new ideas. In certain cases—the *A* lick in Ex. 30, for instance—you arpeggiate a chord two notes at a time.

Rather than holding a barre form, finger only the two notes that are needed at the moment.

The good ol' tried-and-true pick-and-finger technique works best, as it enables you to grab the two notes simultaneously. You also get much better damping capability than with straight flatpicking. Try to play notes on adjacent strings with a pick and your middle finger; use a pick and your ring finger to play intervals that are separated by a string.

Experiment with these licks, and try to incorporate them into your own style—that's where you'll find the *real* payoff.

➤

Double-stop blues

■ We all love to jam on the blues. But there are times when you really want to add spice to your playing by throwing in new techniques. Sometimes I like to *force* this idea—I might, for example, play a solo entirely in double-stops. Not only is this a great chop builder and attention grabber, but it lets you look at soloing in a new light. I also like starting with single-notes, then going to double-stops as a kicker.

I suggest using the pick-and-finger technique that I'm always touting; it's especially helpful for the passages where the notes are separated by one or more strings. Also, the technique helps with right-hand damping and blocking. When playing the example, rest your pick and finger on the two strings you have just played or are about to play. This gives a cleaner sound and lets you grab the strings in a more assertive way. Ex. 35 also features slides, hammer-ons, and pull-offs. Include these techniques as indicated, and experiment with them on your own.

This is some cool stuff. I hope you enjoy it and get a lot of mileage from these ideas.

Ex. 35

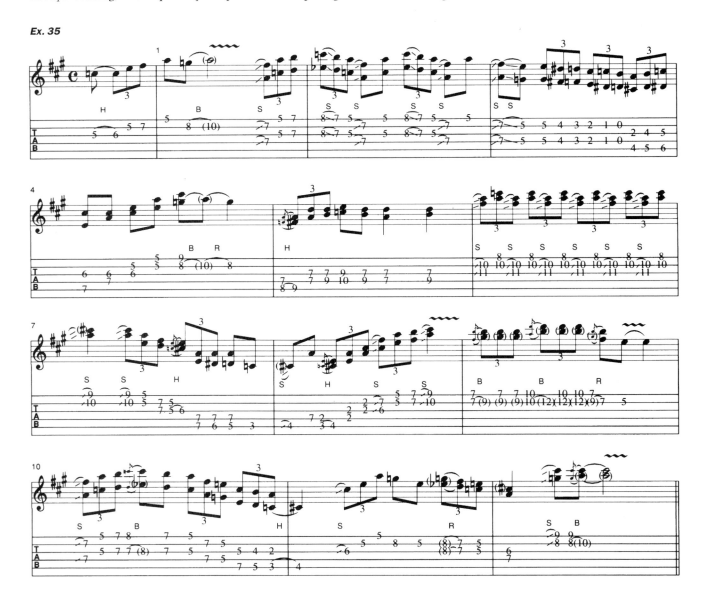

Bluesy double-stops

There's no doubt about it, the blues has arrived again in a big way. But for those of us who view it as a permanent American art form, it never left. A thousand years from now, folks will be listening to blues, just like we now listen to classical music that's centuries old. Future guitarists will still be searching for the perfect vibrato and bend.

I've always used blues as the ideal jamming format and for trying out new ideas. What other structure is better for improvising on your own? As members of western culture—and as Americans in particular—blues seems to be in our blood. Blues and blues-related music are everywhere, and we start hearing it almost as soon as we're born.

Years of experimentation have led me to come up with some cool ways to use double-stops in the blues.

Double- and even triple-stops usually enter the picture as a part of the building process after establishing a single-note phrase or solo.

For two or more notes at a time, I use pick-and-finger technique, which enables me to play accurately and damp unwanted sounds. Rule of thumb: for double-stops on adjacent strings, use the pick and middle finger; for ones that are split by a string, use the pick and ring finger. If you want to get more adventurous when you play double-stops on the first two strings, use your middle and ring fingers, saving the pick for when the third string is called for.

Ex. 36 is a 12-bar chorus that explores double-stops in a lead blues framework. Enjoy, and come up with some ideas on your own.

Ex. 36

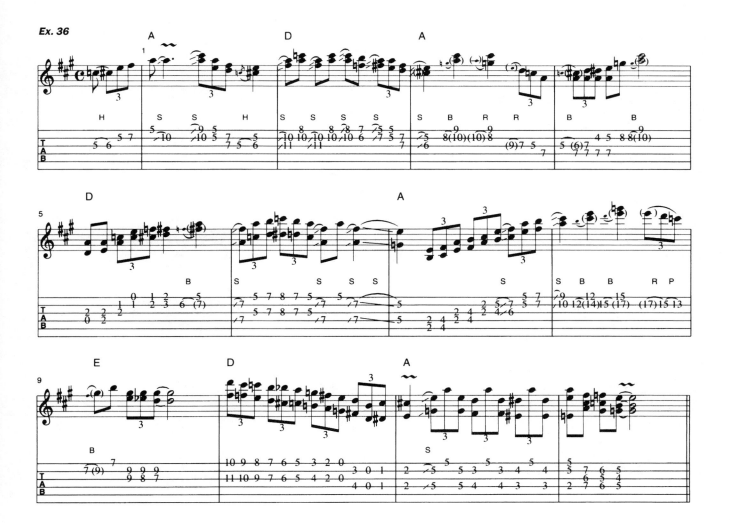

Triple-stop threat

■ I've always favored using more than one string at a time for lead playing, particularly for a country or blues feel. In fact, I've become very interested in the even more challenging triple-stop, which I think can be a viable approach for rhythm and lead guitar.

The licks in Ex. 37 to 40 should give you a good idea of the many ways the triple-stop technique can be used. Right-hand styles can vary; I prefer using a pick and two fingers, while Scotty Anderson, who has got to be the king of the double- and triple-stop, favors holding a thumbpick while playing the higher two strings with the nails of the index and middle fingers. Many jazz players prefer raking right across the three notes simultaneously, lending the chords a special sound and character.

Once you've mastered these, play around with different three-string inversions of what I've shown you and any new triple-stop ideas of your own.

String Bending

Country & pedal steel effects

■ The art of string bending can be one of the most expressive tools in a guitarist's repertoire. While it's great for blues and rock licks, bending strings by no means ends there—one of my favorite uses of this technique is in the country vein.

The primary difference between country and rock or blues string bending is *phrasing*. While a blues lick may be bent up very slowly and unevenly with a great amount of vibrato added at the end, a country bend may be far more mechanical sounding, with a quick resolution to the note, and *no* vibrato. This necessitates learning just how far you need to bend in order to achieve a certain pitch, so that you can get into it and out of it quickly and accurately. That kind of instinctive accuracy comes only with lots and lots of practice.

In country music, the 3rd of a major chord is probably the most common target for a bend. There are others, of course, but for now we'll stick to the positions where you can achieve this major third bend (usually initiated a whole-step below the 3rd of the chord). Another identifying feature of many of these bends is the addition of a harmony note that remains stationary while the bend is moving. This lends a pedal-steel sound to the technique.

In Ex. 1, we're bending to *A*, the 3rd of an *F* major chord, while sustaining the *C,* the 5th of the chord. A good way to visualize the lick before playing it is to think of the bend as a substitute for a hammer-on. Ex. 1 shows the lick both as a hammer-on and a bent note. It is crucial to keep the stationary harmony note firmly anchored while bending the other note. A number of different fingerings will work, so experiment with several—this will develop coordination and strength.

In Ex. 2, we are bending up to the 3rd of a *C* (major) chord. Together, the two positions shown in the prior examples form a grid for licks on the I-IV progression, as in Ex. 3.

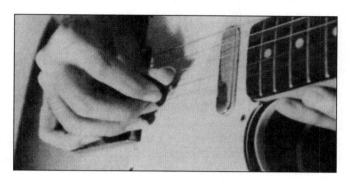

Country players will most often use three or more strings for a steel-like sound, bending one note while keeping two harmony notes stationary. Ex. 4 illustrates this technique. Use your 4th and 3rd fingers for the stationary notes *G* and *C,* and try bending from *D* to *E* with your 1st or 2nd finger.

When doing these pedal steel-like licks, it is helpful to be able to use a combination of pick and two fingers. When picking this way, you get an even, simultaneous attack. The photo shows the hand in ready position for executing the lick in Ex. 4, this time using the pick and fingers technique.

Remember that to get good movement and definition in your string-bending licks, you should keep your fretting fingers *on* the strings as you shift positions, and your picking hand should help damp out unwanted noise while the fretting hand is moving. To play this lick correctly, learn to stop the strings at the point when the bend reaches its highest pitch. The same combination of pick and fingers that plucked the strings comes back down and damps them out, getting ready to play once more in the process.

While far from comprehensive, this is enough to give you a foundation on which to build other country string bending licks.

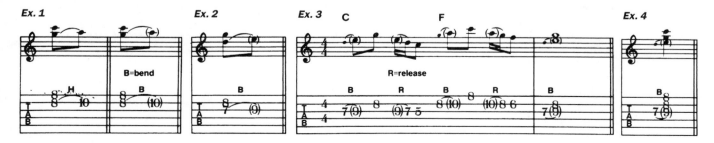

Bending with perfect intonation

■ The biggest problem students encounter is getting or maintaining the proper pitch while bending. The only real solution, I'm afraid, is to use your ear. But it might help if you practice licks in which the bent note is preceded by the same pitch, unbent. That way, the target pitch is fresh in your memory. Luckily, there are many blues and rock licks of this type, and they sound pretty cool!

Some of these licks demonstrate what I'm talking about. Others take a stranger approach: you bend first, release, and then slide, with the same finger that exe-

cuted the bend, up to the note you were bending towards. If done properly, this creates an illusion of two versions of the same note being played on two different strings. The bend-and-release quality almost makes it sound as if you're using a slide.

The bottom line is that as long as the true pitch occurs close to the bend, you can't help but train your ear regarding the proper destination of the bend. And remember, use your extra fingers for support behind the bend.

Half-step bending

Let's look at a specialized form of string bending, namely the half-step variety. When most players think of string bending, they automatically envision bends of at least a whole-step. I'm crazy about those powerful bends, but I also like to emphasize the importance and melodic properties with half-steps in mind. When bending in this manner, you create a much more subtle and melodic approach, and it's a style that works really well within any single-note context. Merle Haggard's sideman, Roy Nichols, is a great example of this style, as are many fine Hawaiian players.

I must reiterate that the bend, even though it's only a half-step in this case, should be done with whatever fingers are available to you *below* the bent note. This also acts as a "block" that pushes the other strings out of the way, and keeps them from creating any unwanted tones. This is especially important when you *return* to the unbent position, as this is when the accidental plucking of notes can occur.

As a starter, I would like you to see how these single-fret bends can work within some of the major pentatonic positions we've been used to. For example, Ex.13 is a run for the key of *A* that exists within the "box" position between the 2nd and 5th frets and uses the bend going from a lowered 5th up to the perfect 5th.

These bends can occur in some of the strangest places, particularly when dealing with the major positions. This is understandable, because one rarely plays some of these dissonant passing tones unless they're involved in something like the bending process. In Ex.14, we see just what I mean, because we're leading up to most of the notes in the scale with a half-step bend.

As a means of improvising, I often like to work within the confines of the *E*-form barre chord and its "additional" notes, such as 6ths, 7ths, 9ths, and lowered 5ths. It's easy to envision these notes as additions to the familiar barre position. Ex.15 shows runs that deal with the 6th of *A (F#)*, in a melodic sense, using half-step bends.

The 9th is also a useful note to use in an "add-on" way, and is illustrated in the group of licks in Ex.16. Take note that many times we are following the bend with a release of the bend, and then a pull-off. Remember that while the bend goes towards you, the pull-off (or left-hand pluck) goes away from you.

Ex. 13

Ex. 14

Ex. 15

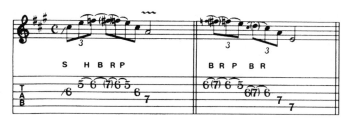

Ex. 16

→

In Ex. 17, we see how we can combine our familiar whole-step bends with some of our new subtle half-steppers to create some different-sounding licks. In these cases, we'll be using all of the top three treble strings.

Ex. 17

Anchoring notes while bending

■ One of the most common problems I encounter when teaching string bending is the student's inability to maintain the pitch of a stationary note while bending another. Fingers like to think and act together, and for this reason, independence and individual control is something you must acquire from lots and lots of playing. Bending is such an obvious example of a technique requiring both strength and independence of movement, because it must utilize so much of the left hand for execution.

A particular movement that gives people trouble is a bent note on the B string with a stationary note on the high E string, as in Ex. 18. The B string should be bent with three fingers, while the pinky holds down the unbent note on the high E string. Try to keep the note on the high E absolutely still, with no change in pitch. You may find that you have to press a little harder to achieve this at first.

Ex. 19 is another common yet hard-to-execute position, this time on the G and B strings. Note that the anchored note is now one fret *above* the bent note and requires even greater control to keep it from wandering from true pitch.

We can also apply this position to the top two strings, adding a *major* third to what was originally a *minor* lick. I like to play it as the final position in a double-stop run, such as the one in Ex. 20.

Ex. 19

Ex. 18

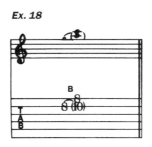

Ex. 20

Ex. 21

Ex. 22

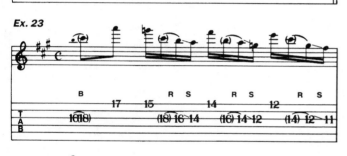

Ex. 23

Using these two-note bend positions in ascending and descending runs can create real showpieces. In Ex. 21, we see how we can move this position around, creating some very melodic licks. Note that in the case of the descending runs, the notes should already be bent up (*silently*) before you release them, to create a "spill-down" effect. If you can't yet hear the pitch of the bend in your head before you play it, you should play the fretted note that it will sound like first, and *then* try to match that pitch with the bend. Eventually, your fingers will develop a feel for just how far to go for each bend.

Ex. 22 illustrates some three-note licks that require two of the notes to be anchored while one note is bent. This is even tougher to do than double-stops, since you have fewer fingers to help the bend along and the fretting fingers must take care of two strings, sometimes on different frets.

In my own soloing, I often use a combination of *G*-string bends and releases with stationary notes on the high *E* string, to create smooth and fast descending runs. In Ex. 23, the index finger must first help the bend, and then it must abandon it to quickly play the descending note on the high *E* string *while* the bend stays in pitch. This is really difficult, especially if you're relying heavily on the index finger for the bend. The trick is to overcompensate with the other fingers that *are* bending, once the index finger leaves the scene. This helps to maintain the pitch of the bend, while the pressure of the fretting fingers remains the same.

Got all of that? Don't worry; it will come eventually. Just make sure to follow all of these steps as methodically as possible, and you'll derive the most benefit from it.

Learning to bend silently

■ The art of bending silently requires that you know in advance just how far a note must be bent *before* it is released. Many players always bend up to a note—as opposed to having it bent to begin with—and this can get fairly monotonous. Imagine a singer always slurring up into a note, never hitting it right on the money—it would drive you crazy!

I love the idea of having notes bent ahead of time. It gives you so many options of phrasing and expression. It also gives you a unique and subtle vibrato, since the vibrato is actually created by a bend-and-release action. This gives the vibrato a more plaintive, singing quality. Sometimes I bend a note silently—with no audible trace of the note from which the bend originates—just so I can get this type of vibrato. It also works great if you sound a regular fretted note, and *then* play the silently bent vibrating note; this creates an interesting before-and-after effect. Silent bends also work great with double-stops. (Usually, you bend with two fingers while a third finger plays another note on another string.)

All the licks in Ex. 24 involve whole-step (two-fret) bends. The indication "silent bend" is used to distinguish the bends in which you never hear the pitch of the note you're actually fingering, as opposed to the usual sliding-into-the-note type of bend.

This is an important exercise for coordinating ear-training and finger memory. Eventually, you should be able to pick up your guitar and silently bend a note up in perfect tuning ever time. This takes practice, but doesn't everything? I venture to guess that you will probably bend sharp at first, but after a while your fingers will seem to have built-in "presets" telling them just how far is enough.

Ex. 24

play simultaneously

Basic double-note bends

■ Let's examine the fine points of *multi*-string bending. There are rarely times when you must control the strings with as much accuracy as in multi-string bends, and to do this takes a lot of practice. Each string has its own thickness and tension; therefore, there are times when you must exert different amounts of pressure to achieve bends of equal length. This brings up one of the technique's oddest yet most important quirks: two strings of different thicknesses can also receive the same pressure to create bends of *different* values.

This shows that double-note bends can actually be easier than most people think, and that your fingers

→

needn't be "thinking" so independently. To show what I mean, Ex. 25—a double-note bend in *A* on both the *B* and *G* strings—must be made to sound as if the two notes, both on the 7th fret, go to the 8th and 9th frets in pitch. Fortunately, since the *G* string is looser than the *B*, it can receive the same pressure as the *B* string, but go up a whole-step while the *B* goes up only a half-step.

This will take some getting used to, since it's so easy to assume that bends of different lengths must receive different amounts of pressure. You must work on controlling your hand, and train your ear to recognize when the bends have reached the right pitches. For example, the bend in Ex. 26, where the notes must go up an equal distance, is far more difficult because your fingers must think more independently.

As we go to the higher strings and involve the high *E*, its tension presents greater difficulty, and for some (yours truly included), can make the bending process a bit more of a strain. Ex. 27 once again features a whole-step jump on one string while the other goes up only a half-step. Be sure to make the high *E* string reach the proper pitch.

Chuck Berry has always been one of the masters of double-note bends, and though his licks lack the sophistication of going to varying lengths, he still combines them and straight playing with amazing speed and finesse. A Chuck Berry bend usually consists of two notes, on adjacent strings and common frets, both bent up a half- or whole-step. The pair of licks in Ex. 28 illustrates some of the more familiar positions we hear Chuck Berry bending in.

Ex. 29, in the Chuck Berry style, will help you to "get in and out" of these bending positions, quickly going from bends to normal fretted and barred notes.

Ex. 25

Ex. 26

Heat up your solos with double-note bends

■ In my lead playing, I like to use several basic positions involving two-note half-step bends. These often include a third, anchored note that acts as an equalizer. When the two notes are bent, they usually form a chord with this third note. This gives your ear something to "shoot for," and helps your fingers learn just how far they should bend ahead of time. Ex. 30 shows some of the double-note bends. Try to achieve the proper pitch with the bend. Note: They might require different amounts of pressure from each finger, so watch out!

One of my favorite applications of this style is to create ascending and descending runs that not only include the bends, but also more repetitions of the same position. An experienced guitarist will probably recognize the rather standard and worn-out "blues turnaround" positions as likely candidates for updating with double-note bends. Some of these great licks are included in Ex. 31. I also like to move through chord changes with bends, often resolving to a different chord at the end of the lick.

To play the bends notated in the tablature in the first part of Ex. 30 (and all similar examples), pluck the 5 on the first string at the same time that you play the 4 and the 5 on the second and third strings, respectively.

Ex. 31 has a group of runs that illustrate the "turnaround" style of double-note bends. Please note that many times you're required to have the bend up to pitch *before* the notes are sounded. Then you begin to release the bend and create the rest of the run.

In the group of patterns in Ex. 32, we see how we can utilize the same technique to move through chord changes. Try to experiment with this technique, shifting and moving positions as much as possible. Look for places where there are repetitions of positions such as these to help you create new licks.

Practice these runs carefully, and try to bend as cleanly as possible. This will especially help you in the runs that require not only a bend, but also a release of the bend and a sustained slide after the notes have been played.

Ex. 32

More double-note bends

■ It's important to know how string gauge can affect two-note bends, especially when each string is stretched a different distance. For example, to bend the *G* string up a whole-step and the adjacent *B* string up only a half-step when both notes are at the same fret—a common situation—your fingers don't have to act as independently as you might think. Since the *B* string is more taut than the *G* string, applying the same force to each results in a half-step bend on one and a whole-step bend on the other. When this type of bend is correctly executed, the distance between the stretched strings remains about the same as when the strings are relaxed.

Ex. 33 shows a two-note bend in which one string is raised a half-step and the other is raised a whole-step. Exerting the same pressure on each string should produce the desired sound. In this instance, there's enough room to stretch the strings toward either side of the fingerboard.

Ex. 34 shows five of my favorite double-note bends. In the third lick, the higher note is raised a whole-step and the lower note is raised a half, while the opposite occurs in all the others.

Ex. 33

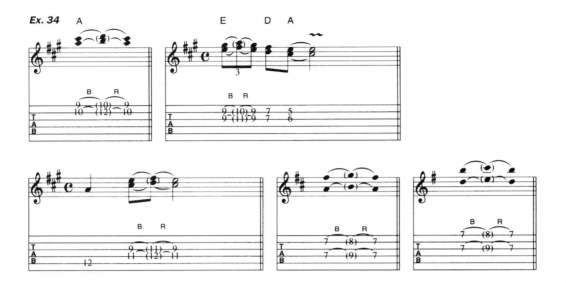

Ex. 34

Pedal-steel sounds with double-string bends

■ When you're into imitating the pedal-steel sound on guitar, you're always trying to think of new ways to play bends as substitutions for conventionally fretted notes, and multiple-note bends are bound to grab you sooner or later. The technique is also applicable to blues and rock, but the pedal-steel-style approach can be the most challenging—and rewarding—because of the precision it requires.

Remember what we've discovered about double-string bends: just because you must push two strings of different thicknesses across different distances, don't assume that you have to use each finger completely independently. It's the different string gauges that determine each string's unique bending properties. Of course, some strings bend easier than others. If I wanted to bend the *G* string up a whole-step while bending the high *E* string a half-step (Ex. 35), the same amount of pressure applied to each string would do the trick—the high *E* is tighter and harder to bend than the relatively pliable *G*.

Still, getting the right pitches when two strings are involved is no easy task. One problem is simple *space;*

sometimes double bends on adjacent strings allow barely enough room for your fingers. Ex. 36 shows one of my favorite pedal-steel-style licks. If the note on the *G* string isn't bent far enough, the *D* string will be bent over the *G* string and cancel its note.

Ex. 35

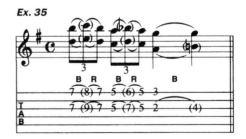

Ex. 36

Double-note bends make great substitutions for otherwise mundane and repetitious descending runs (Ex. 37). These sorts of bends may be either half-steps or whole-steps, but in either case the strings require equal pressure. These licks sound the fretted notes before the bends occur, which sets you up by letting you hear the target pitch before you bend up to it. Also, the connecting slides add to the overall smoothness of the runs. Try them out, have fun, and remember to keep those pitches true.

Ex. 37

Three-note bends & beyond

■ Though double-note bends are quite difficult, they are familiar to most fairly advanced players, and these guitarists rarely venture beyond the two-note realm in their bending escapades. Well, I'm here to change all that—at least for the time being.

You know I enjoy bending strings, but if you have listened to my records, you'll note the extensive use of three-, four- and even five-note bends in my solos and back-up parts. So far, I have discussed how you must stretch different strings varying distances for many two-note bends. This, however, is rarely the case when bending whole chords because the effect we want to get is more of a bend-and-return or release-of-a-bend sound.

Generally speaking, you want to look for groups of notes or chords that have nice, clustered formations that are easy to "grab." Because of this, I like to bend *D* and *D7* forms, other 7th forms, and 9th chords. In every case, except for chords that have notes on the high *E* string, you should make these bends *away* from yourself. This gives you a lot more leverage, and you can grip the neck with your thumb while the rest of your hand pulls down and away in a pivoting motion.

Keep in mind that these bends are really not as difficult as they seem. As long as you can keep strength in the bend, and not let the strings overlap each other, you should be in pretty good shape. The bend in Ex. 38 is based on the 9th-chord form, and involves all four fingers of the fretting hand. First, start by playing the notes, and then bend them all *down*, applying even pressure to each string. Ideally, what we want is the effect of a *half-step* bend.

Ex. 38

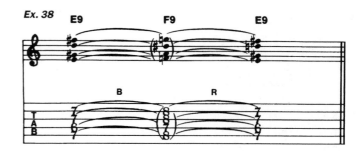

➡

Next, in Ex. 39, we take the same bend and make it part of an *E9* to *D9* change, something I like to do when reaching this part of a blues progression. Here we are first sounding the normal fretted *E9* chord, and then sneaking down one fret below it and silently bending up to something approximating the *E9*, so we can then release the bend to a *D#9*, and finally *slide* that position down one fret to the *D9*.

In the following form of the 9th chord (Ex. 40), the same four fingers do the bending, but the turned-around position of this chord makes it just a little more difficult to get a good pivoting motion happening. Try it slowly at first, making sure to keep the strings from overlapping each other.

The position in Ex. 41 is one of my favorite discoveries because it takes one three-note chord and turns it into a completely new chord quite naturally with the bend. In this case, we are taking an *A7* position and, with the bend, actually turning it into a *D* major chord! You'll find that this kind of lick lends itself to the melodic qualities of a solo quite readily, and can be further explored by playing one note at a time with either a pick-and-finger technique or by individually picking the notes.

In Ex. 42, our most difficult three-note bend, based on the *D* chord form, we must bend *towards* us. This brings the chord up a whole-step, but to a *minor* form. Here, we're taking an *A* chord up to a *Bm* with the bend.

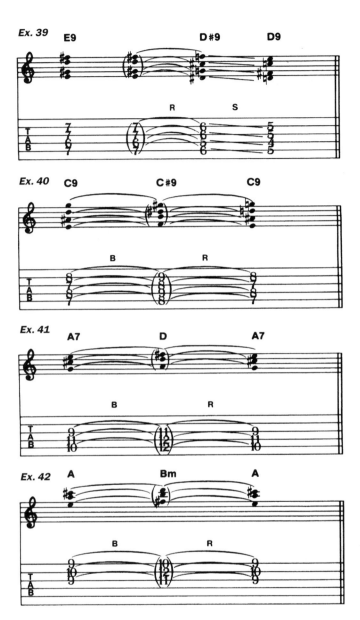

Combining half- & whole-step bends

■ Let's try an interesting twist on string bending: licks that combine whole- and half-step bends. This is an important exercise, because it teaches you some very subtle bending discipline, and it helps train your ear. These days you hear so many guitarists, some good ones, who simply have no idea which notes to bend and how far! I think it may be because some heavy metal players use such slinky strings that they don't have much of a sure "feel" for bends, and also that locking tremolo units can play havoc with a bent note, forcing you to bend it

→

farther than normal. I know I've occasionally been stuck playing this kind of a guitar at a jam session, and man, it can sure ruin my day!

Anyway, no ruined days here, just some nice, tasty bend licks that'll really have your guitar talkin'. Remember to pay close attention to the notes and num-bers in parentheses, because they tell you how far the notes should be bent. Also keep in mind that these are strictly half- or whole-step bends, nothing in between; you need truly accurate bends to make these licks come to life. Have fun bending away, and I hope you come up with some nice combo bend licks of your own.

Ex. 43

Country bending in the open position

■ Surely one of the guitar's most benevolent locations is the great and well-known open position of *G*. There is a wide array of country licks and bends that I enjoy fooling around with in *G*, and I've found that the pick-and-fingers technique—or for that matter, straight fingerpicking—is certainly a more appropriate approach for this style than standard flatpicking. Pick-and-fingers affords you greater damping flexibility and makes the many "split-string" two- and three-note licks much easier.

One problem with making bends this low on the neck is that there's nowhere near the amount of slack in the string as there would be at, say, the 7th fret. Therefore, most of these licks require a bit more of the old "chokeroo" to get up to proper pitch. Many players shy away from bends in this area for this very reason—letting the middle of the neck be the "safe" location for bends. However, the open strings do at least give you the option, both musically and physically of "bailing out" of a bending situation that's too severe, without making things discordant. If you have trouble getting your bends up to the correct pitch, first play the note in parentheses after the note to hear what the bend *should* sound like; then try to match the note with your bend while the pitch is still fresh in your ear.

The open-*G* pedal steel-ish lick in Ex. 44 is to be played in an almost banjo-like fashion with the pick and fingers. Be sure to bend the note up with the index as well as the middle finger, and try to maintain that bent pitch while playing the rest of the pattern.

When playing the next lick in Ex. 45, be sure to hold down the notes on the *B* and high *E* strings while all the hammering and bending is taking place on the *D* and *G* strings. This will enable you to create a nice droning effect while single-note work is being laid down over it.

It's a little tougher to make the bend on the *B* string but well worth the effort. Ex. 46 is one lick that creates a nice effect with the use of a minor seventh and a cascading bent note.

In the next run in Ex. 47 we combine bending on both the *B* and *G* strings. It may take a while before you can make a smooth transition between the two.

Ex. 48 is definitely one of my more off-the-wall open-position bends. I like bending on the low strings a lot, but it seems that besides Duane Eddy, this has become a lost art! Note: By the end of the lick, you're actually bending up a half-step on the low *E* string while it harmonizes with the open *D* and *G*.

Ex. 44

Ex. 45

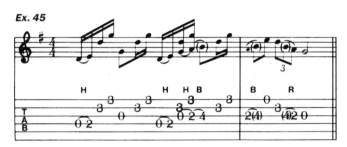

Ex. 46

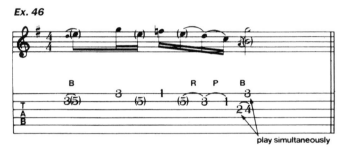

Ex. 47

Ex. 48

In Ex. 49 I stray a bit from the open bends to create a bassy, steel-like effect, but the open harmony strings are still employed.

Ex. 49

Bending on the lower strings

■ Many guitarists shy away from bending the lower strings, but there's truly a wealth of great sounds using this technique. In fact, they're often easier to execute than their high-string counterparts. Of course, when bending on the low *E*, *A*, and *D* strings, we must almost always bend away from us (toward the high *E* string). In the case of this kind of bend, we gain strength from the pivoting motion our hand makes as we bend down and away. We gain further strength from our thumb coming over the edge of the fingerboard and applying added pressure in the direction that counts. It also serves a bonus role of damping out any unwanted accidental tones on the lower strings that may not be involved directly with the bend.

If you want to hear some of these kinds of bends at their twangiest, listen to Duane Eddy. As I've stressed before, you must help the bend along with as many other fingers as are available behind the actual bending finger. This also serves the additional role as a damper of unwanted tones, particularly when the bend is released back to its "relaxed" position.

First, let's look at some real twangy licks that involve notes bent on the low *E* string (Ex. 50). This string is the loosest of all, so be careful not to *over*bend as so many guitarists do when they first try these. Observe that some of the licks keep the bend up to pitch, while others use a bend and release.

Ex. 50

play simultaneously

The *A* string is also great for bends, but since it's a bit stiffer than the low *E*, it can present more problems. It's also crowded between two strings, unlike the low *E*, and that means that damping is even more important in this more hazardous situation. Note how some of the licks in Ex. 51 combine bends on both the *A* and low *E* strings.

Ex. 51

The *D* is perhaps the most difficult string to bend on the guitar (Ex. 52). It's got many strikes against it: it's in the middle of the fingerboard, and it's thin but still wound, which definitely makes it the tightest string to bend. (Those who have ever tried long bends on a wound *G* string know what I'm talking about!) Nevertheless it is useful, and if you can execute bends on this elusive string, you've got something special happening!

Ex. 52

Open-position rolls & country bends

■ Open-position rolls and bends can be used to produce a great pedal-steel effect. But open-position bends can be a bit more difficult than those played in the middle of the neck, so you'll have to use extra pressure to get them in tune. Remember what I've preached all along: use as many fingers as are available *behind* the bending finger. Also, when you bend towards the low *E* string, you can use your index finger to help push the other strings out of the way of the bent string—this helps eliminate unwanted "clangs" when you return the note to its unbent position. In many of these licks, you must sustain a fretted note while executing the bend, maintaining the pitch of the bend without knocking the unbent notes out of tune.

The keys of *G* and *A* offer the most possibilities for open-position bending. Ex. 53 to 56 are in *G*, and they feature some banjo-type rolls. Make sure you arch your left-hand fingers so that the open strings ring out freely.

While these four examples combine bends with higher-pitched unbent notes, the next four licks (Ex. 57 to 60), all in *A*, require you to bend against a sustained *lower* note. Ex. 60, which Eric Johnson showed me, is a real doozy—it's one of the trickiest pedal-steel-type licks I

➤

know. It requires a "straight-over-the-neck," jazz-style left-hand position, because you must simultaneously fret a note on the *D* string, bend the note at the 4th fret of the *G* string *downwards,* and slide your pinky from the 4th to the 5th fret on the high *E* string. This coordinated bend-and-slide action creates a great simulation of two notes being bent at once. The hardest part is making sure that the bent third string doesn't push the first string clear off the fingerboard—you'll see what I mean when you try it.

Ex. 53

Ex. 54

Ex. 55

Ex. 56

Ex. 57

Ex. 58

Ex. 59

Ex. 60

Bending in open positions

■ Obviously, when someone gets heavily into string bending, most of his experiments take place up the neck in the closed, more lead guitar-oriented positions. I've been bending strings all over the place for quite some time now, and I've found some really nice "closed-position" bends that exist lower on the neck; these are based upon open chord positions.

One of the primary reasons why many of us stay away from open-position bends is that we think it's too hard to bend this far down the neck, that there isn't enough slack behind the string to help the bend along. Well, that's really not true, and in fact many open-position bends are very easy. Certainly where chord-like bends are con-

cerned (in which certain other notes must be sustained over the bend itself), these positions hold a definite edge over similar "closed" positions.

In the positions in Ex. 61, you'll note my usage of the bend-release, pull-off pattern. This lends itself perfectly to the open-string positions, as we can now pull-off on a nicely ringing open string without having to create the usual "anchor" note utilized during closed pull-off licks. Most of the licks involve the major third in one way or another, such as bending up to it, or as a suspended-fourth type of bend that releases to the major third.

Remember to use as many fingers as possible to help bend the strings, and you'll be all right!

"Overbends" in blues & rock

■ Overbending is a topic that is rarely dealt with properly. By "overbending," I'm simply referring to bends that are greater than a whole-step, and which are specifically used for extra emotional emphasis. We've all heard these kinds of bends, particularly in the playing of blues artists such as Eric Clapton, Otis Rush, Albert King, Buddy Guy, and B.B. King. They require a strong left hand that is also capable of an intense vibrato technique. I often find myself "cheating" these bends by simply moving up a fret when I wish to bend, therefore keeping the actual bend a whole-step rather than a step-and-a-half. This is fine when the note you wish to reach is the priority, but the sheer emotional *strain* effect can only be had when you put some muscle into it and make the full sweep of the overbend.

Most of these extreme bends are found easiest on the *G* and *B* strings, and should bend *towards* you. This gives you more power, and most important, more *room!* The photo shows an overbend on the *G* string. Note how my 2nd and 1st fingers are helping the 3rd finger to bend the string, while the index finger serves the added function of pushing the other strings out of the way. This means that you won't be bending *under* the fat strings—an oft-made mistake by even experienced players—and there won't be any "clangs" when you release the bend and return to your normal position.

Ex. 62, a bending lick in *A*, represents what I consider to be the classic Chicago blues overbend position. Keep in mind that the note you're going to eventually reach is the *7th* of the chord (*G*), and that the bend should really feel as if it's being stretched to its limits—right until it reaches the desired pitch. Ex. 63 is the same bend in a higher position, on the *E* string. (Be careful not to break the string!)

Ex. 64, on the *B* string, comes out of the B.B. King "box" position. You hear this one a lot in the playing of Clapton, Stevie Ray Vaughan, and Billy Gibbons. Be sure to make the bend a part of the overall phrase as I've written it.

Ex. 62

Ex. 63

Ex. 64

Finally, Ex. 65 incorporates several of the overbends into a somewhat cohesive (I hope!) little ditty. Have fun experimenting with these; I'm sure you'll find lots of new ones on your own. Just be sure to make them musical, rather than just bending away in a hit-or-miss fashion. It's easy to get carried away, especially if you're using very light-gauge strings.

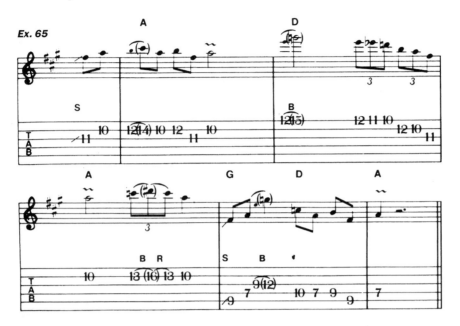

Ex. 65

Bending with your 1st finger

■ There are many instances when an index finger bend becomes the only true way for the lead guitarist to express what must be said at the moment. We are all familiar with bends that require two or even three fingers to execute (though many of us wrongly try these with one finger). These are always 2nd- or 3rd-finger bends, and they almost always require the extra push that the other fingers can supply.

In blues we often find that we have no choice but to use the 1st finger when the note we must bend is at a lower point on the fretboard than the other notes of the lick. The most common use of this kind of bend usually occurs within a standard blues "box" position, when resolving from a minor to a major 3rd. It's important to note here that these index-finger bends must utilize a pivoting motion off of the side of the neck, similar to the way we create a B.B. King-style pivoting vibrato.

Therefore, it is a bend down away from you, towards the high *E* string. In fact, the only time we must bend in the opposite direction is (obviously) when it occurs on the high *E* string itself. In that case, it's a bend towards us, without using the pivot approach.

The first group of licks (Ex. 66) uses the index finger to bend from the minor 3rd to the major 3rd in several positions. Try to get your finger used to just how far it must bend the note on the various strings.

In the next group of exercises (Ex. 67), we must use the pivot action to even greater lengths, as we are now creating a two-fret bend and release. This is commonly heard in the playing of the big blues benders such as B.B. and Albert King, Otis Rush, and Buddy Guy.

There are also times, as in Ex. 68, when I use these bends to help a musical passage along, making the lick reach for a chord that we are just passing through. This is

→

a particularly useful part of index-finger bending, as it keeps us from having to shift positions too often for different chord changes.

Experiment on your own with these. Index-finger bends, particularly of the one-fret length, are applicable anywhere on the neck, and can really spice up otherwise typical musical passages.

Ex. 66

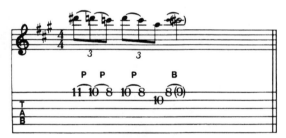

Ex. 67

Ex. 68

Combining bends with stretches

■ Over the years I've come up with a lot of interesting positions on the neck that combine the use of bends with other fretted notes involving rather extreme stretches. The stretches themselves aren't so difficult, but they are made so because a great deal of the hand is committed to making the bend possible, leaving very little in the way of true flexibility for the hand's muscles. This combination of bending and stretching is, however, a great tool to have, and it's certainly a fine exercise for getting your left hand in better shape.

The important thing to keep in mind while practicing these bends is that you still must use another finger behind the bending finger to help the bend along. This at first may seem to tie your hand up too much, but in actuality it's making it easier for you to execute the lick than by keeping the pitch up with one finger. The addition of having to stretch another note would even further weaken the one-finger bend. Of course, another great thing about this technique is that it gives you some intriguing harmonies and positions usually thought impossible when bending. They definitely catch your attention, that's for sure!

Ex. 69 presents a group of licks utilizing this technique. Notice that some require the bend and the stretched note to be sustained together, while at other times you need only to catch the stretched note momentarily, not putting as much strain on your fretting hand.

These licks, of course, only represent a small part of what you can do within this technique, so feel free to try some of your own outlandish ideas. You never know what will happen.

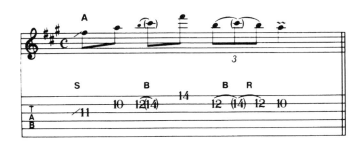

Ex. 69

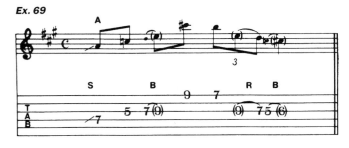

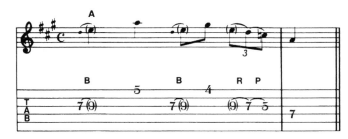

More stretching & bending

■ I've always advocated the "get in and get out fast" approach to bending—no matter what type of bend is required, you commit your entire hand to the bending process, letting your thumb come over the neck and using your extra fingers to help bend and damp—the whole nine yards.

But some single-note runs require such big stretches that there literally isn't enough time to "get in and get out" of the traditional blues-style bends. We must assume the straight-over-the-fingerboard classical-style position to accommodate the stretches, which makes bending a lot tougher because of the position's lack of leverage. But it *can* be done, and even if you'll always be a blues-style bender, it's good to have some of these techniques up your sleeve.

This new approach requires a lot more strength from the fingers themselves, since you don't have the same amount of opposing pressure from the thumb—though there should be some—and your fingers are at more of a right angle to the string than before. It's still advisable to use extra fingers to help push up the bent note whenever possible.

In Ex. 70, the required stretches leave little time to go into the indicated bends, so practice them slowly at first. Hope you enjoy them, and that they open some new doors in your playing.

Ex. 70

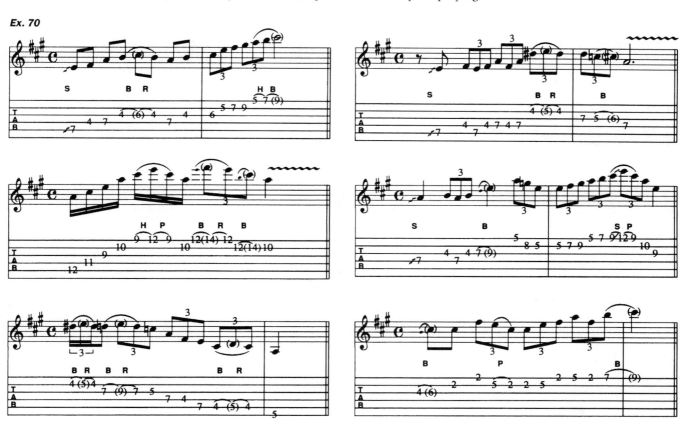

Combination bends

■ Bends can be integrated into fast single-note phrases that combine various techniques. Let's cover some basics that facilitate mastering this difficult style.

The trickiest aspect of Ex. 71 to 74 is the bend/release/slide pattern, which requires a strong left hand and enough sustain to enable the note to ring throughout. If you support a bend with two fingers, the helping finger often needs to leave quickly to do something else.

Extraneous string noise that prevents you from achieving a clean single-note effect can be eliminated with right- and/or left-hand damping.

These examples employ either the *E* and *B* or the *B* and *G* strings. Even though similar patterns are played on these pairs, their gauges result in a distinctly different sound.

Finally, be sure that your bends are in tune!

Ex. 71

Ex. 72

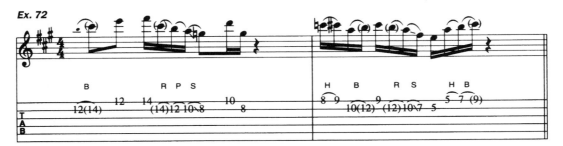

Ex. 73

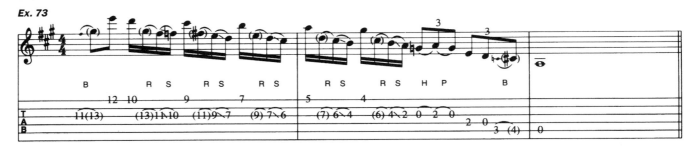

Ex. 74

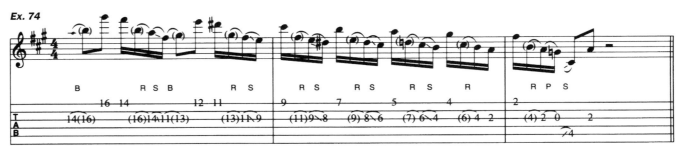

Steady-bass & bends

■ John Sebastian once called me a "string-bending fool"; I can never get enough of that slinky-sounding stuff! One idea I've presented at a number of clinics is using bends in conjunction with a steady bass. While this approach enters fingerpicking's domain, it enables you to sustain bends while the bass locks into a rhythmic groove.

With normal lead playing, it's important to support the bending finger with as many other fingers as possible, which facilitates pushing the string. This also holds true when you combine bends with a steady bass. However, there's an added challenge: to avoid cutting the bass notes short, you need to bend the string toward the fingerboard's treble side.

I call the position for the bend the "B.B. King-esque pivot"; it's often used to produce a quick vibrato. The left hand pivots from the lower portion of the 1st finger that contacts the side of the neck, pulling the string away from low *E*. This also works for straight fingerpicking, where your good old thumb plays the basses and your three fingers perform the lead work. Although the pick-and-fingers approach sacrifices a finger, you gain the pick's edge and bite.

The 12-bar blues in *A* (Ex. 75) utilizes three open bass strings. Open *A* leaves a fair amount of room for treble-side bends, while open *D* only allows half-step stretches. Low *E*, however, offers room in either direction. (The *B* string generally can't be bent toward the treble side with any consequence; but with a steady low *E*, it can be stretched toward the bass side a whole-step or more!)

Feel your way through the piece, and you'll see what I'm getting at. Keep those bass notes nice and steady, and you'll be in good shape.

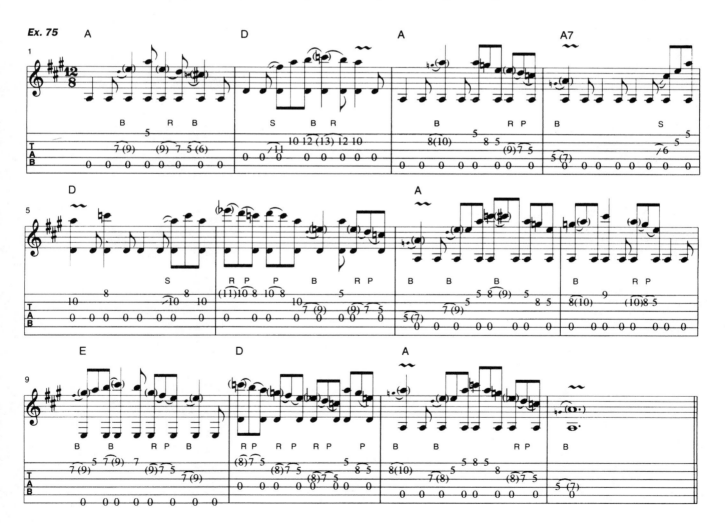

Ex. 75

Skills and Techniques

Pivoting exercises for both hands

■ Throughout previous lessons, the only "pivot" I've referred to has been in conjunction with the kind of B.B. King-like vibrato I recommend, where the left hand pivots off of the side of the neck to produce the proper movement needed for the vibrato. In the case of this lesson, however, the pivot is actually a musical situation in which one note is held down while the others move. This is an excellent power and accuracy builder for your right-hand picking, because it forces you to work very quickly within relatively tight spaces and teaches you economy of motion. It's important to maintain an up-and-down picking motion for these pieces, and to start them relatively slowly and build up speed as you go along. The idea is really to play them fast, and in fact, you'll find that for many of you, the faster you play this style, the easier it is to execute. The technique is hard to demonstrate slowly, since I only use it when playing rapidly.

Be sure to let the pick "dance" over the strings for these, since it has to jump strings many times. This requires a very relaxed and loose wrist, but at the same time, great accuracy. I'm quite sure that once you've worked these into your style, the benefits will be quite apparent.

The first group of exercises in Ex. 1 deals with a pivot off of the *B* string, while the moving notes are on the high *E*. You could experiment with using a barre with the first finger, but I wouldn't recommend that you waste a lot of energy by maintaining it throughout the entire lick.

The next bunch of licks in Ex. 2 involves a jump from the *G* string to the high *E* string, and tests your accuracy a bit more than the previous group. Remember to start the *G*-string notes with a downstroke, while using an upstroke for the notes on the high *E* string.

Ex. 1

Ex. 2

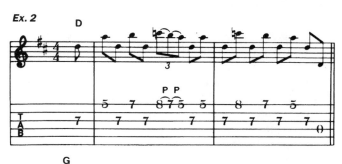

Ex. 3 mixes things up a bit, in that the exercises pivot between the *G* and *E* strings while throwing in an occasional *B* string note, as well. I encourage you to use these to find some of your own pivot licks, for the possibilities are truly infinite. You'll see that once the technique is under your control, the ideas will really start to flow. So practice and practice, but have fun while you're doing it. And most of all, keep those ears and fingers open to new ideas!

Ex. 3

Left-hand independence

■ Very few guitarists actually work on developing better independence for each left-hand finger. Instead, they go on and on playing basically what they're comfortable with, letting their fingers fall into all kinds of ruts by doing the same kinds of things all the time. Getting the fingers to move independently is the mark of many of today's great players, and if you listen to guys such as Steve Morse and Vinnie Moore, you can hear the payoff of this kind of practice.

Many of these kinds of exercises make little musical sense; they're primarily technical, almost abstract ways to use the fretboard as a place to work out certain physical problems. Rarely in "real-life" playing do these sequences come up, but your performance will certainly show the effects once you've done a lot of this kind of practicing. Notice that in some of these exercises I've deliberately made some rather strange jumps from string to string, in ways that you may not be used to. This is, of course, purposeful, and it will further enhance your technique.

Ex. 4 is designed to familiarize your hand with using two fingers at a time on different strings. In other words, the first two notes, say, on the low *E* string are played with the 1st and 3rd fingers, while the next two

notes are played by the 2nd and 4th fingers. I've worked it out so they at least play the frets that fall naturally under them, because the exercise gives you enough problems as it is! Remember to use alternate picking (down-up, down-up, etc.).

In Ex. 5 we use the ever-popular "chromatic" style to help bring out more independence. This time we're breaking it up between two different kinds of three-note patterns. Try to eventually play this one briskly and with accurate right-hand action. Remember, start the lower three notes with the index finger and the higher three with the 2nd finger.

Ex. 6 is rather strange and difficult, as it involves the 4th finger during each section. The only variable is which finger frets the first note of each two-note pattern. We alternate—1st-4th, 2nd-4th, 1st-4th, etc.

These are just some ideas. I'm sure you'll be able to come up with countless other similar exercises on your own—maybe some that aren't as boring! Anyway, I hope you don't mind too much my little venture into techno-land. After all, nobody said it would be *all* fun!

➤

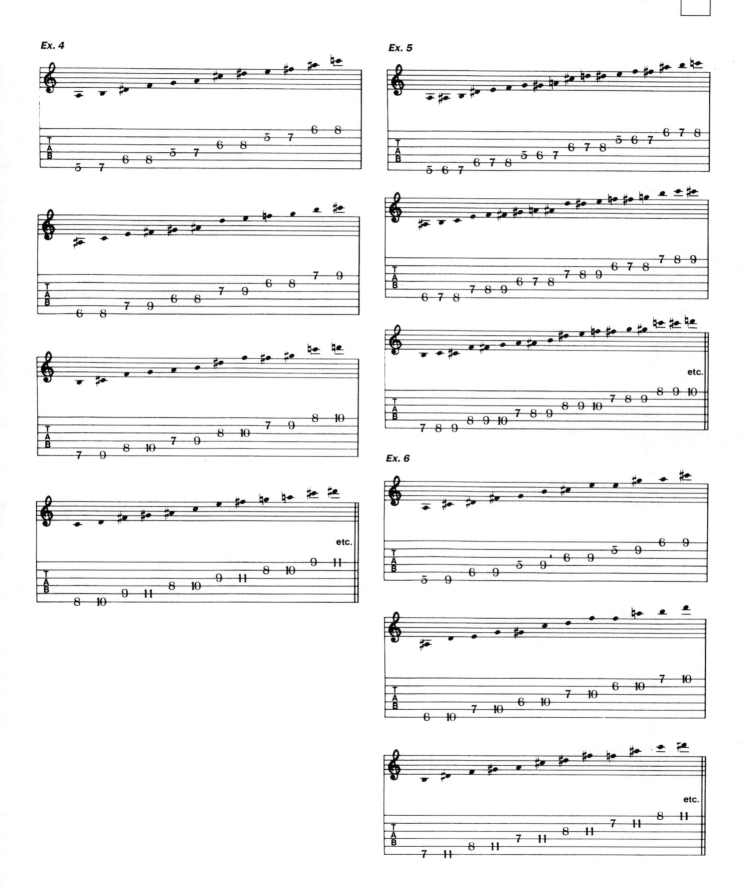

Shifting positions smoothly

■ Many guitarists have come to me with the complaint that they can play lots of licks, but that they simply can't properly connect them in various positions on the neck. Obviously there are many exercises and scales to practice in order to gain expertise in shifting positions, but they can still leave you in a rut when it comes to really putting this technique to use in a real-life situation.

Many times audible slides between notes are the best means of shifting positions, but even better are the silent slides and shifts that occur so inconspicuously that the listener perceives no position change at all. In the case of these kinds of licks, you must really know where you're going beforehand; otherwise you may end up in big trouble. Of course, on the other hand you shouldn't really try any difficult jumps like that unless you do know where you're headed, and what the fingerboard has in store for you. Most of all, one must be thinking ahead of what is being played. When people come to me with a problem of

connecting licks or shifting positions, what they're really complaining about is a lack of fretboard knowledge, resulting in a lack of improvisational skills.

Be that as it may, let's at least look at some ways to help develop this fretboard connecting. In Ex. 7, an elongated version of a major pentatonic scale, we see how very fast, audible slides can help you shift positions very rapidly. Take note that these are just heard as slides, not as two notes that are connected, even though they do start at the last note played before you begin sliding to the next.

In Ex. 8, we see the lower blues position suddenly connected with what I've always called the B.B. King box position of the major pentatonic scale. This slide should always occur with the second finger, as it allows the others to fall in very naturally to their respective positions. This lick is especially useful when the progression goes to the IV chord.

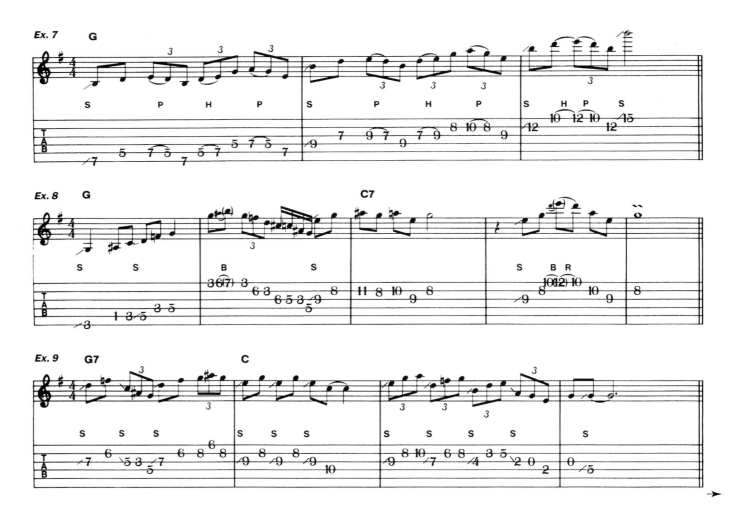

Often the answer to "Where do I go next?" is lying right beneath your fingertips. Many two-note positions, for example, can be shifted all over the place to apply to new situations and chords. Ex. 9 is a case where the same two-finger configuration moves a few times to bring you into different musical passages. I hope you enjoy it, and please experiment with this idea on your own. It will help you open some of the limitless possibilities of the fingerboard. Remember: think ahead!

Big stretches

■ There are a lot of us who use rather conventional positions for lead guitar and rely on the very popular and somewhat overplayed technique of right-hand tapping to get notes that are off in the stratosphere. That's okay, and in many cases it's the only way of getting to these notes. There are, however, a lot of more traditional "stretch" positions I like to use in blues and rock playing that are of a similar nature to the now-familiar right-hand "tap-ons."

Many of these positions came as a result of experimenting within the traditional blues "box" scales, and the need to branch out a bit within them. Since I'm an unchangeable three-fingered player, my left-hand pinky is really too weak to play a lot of these—so I've actually been making four-, five-, and six-fret stretches with my 3rd finger all this time! I do this by simply letting my finger creep up the side of the fretboard and catch the given

note almost from underneath it. You can try this method, too, but I'm sure that most of you would prefer to use your pinky for these licks. It's important that you build up your pinky's strength, and these exercises can be great, particularly in the more demanding performing situations, where acrobatics and flash also count.

The pattern in Ex. 10 is a series of left-hand stretches combined with rapid pull-offs. Note the changing of the chords implied by the licks. These all employ a partial index-finger barre over the top two strings, and again, you may try either the 3rd finger or the pinky to make the long stretch.

We can now use the same index-finger barre on the high *E* and *B* strings, but the stretch pull-offs can occur on the *B* instead of the *E*. In Ex. 11 the pattern also includes a nice two-note hammer-on going up on the *B* string.

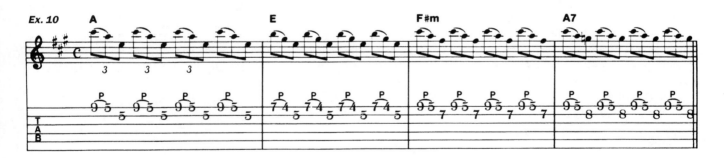

Once we've gotten used to playing these stretches in relatively stationary positions, it's another whole challenge to try moving them up the fingerboard, especially while not breaking stride or losing a beat. This simply improves with practice, as the patterns and positions become well-established in your mind's eye before they are played. Take special note that the positions in Ex. 12, while played one right after the other, are not exactly the same, and they involve subtle changes in positioning on your part.

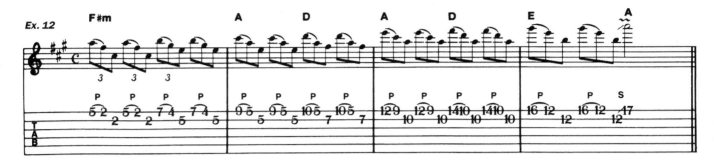

Alternating with open strings

■ From the coldest classical to the wildest rock guitar, the flashy use of open-string notes combined with fretted ones can make for some of the more challenging licks. It's another of those "illusionary" techniques that makes it seem like there's more going on than there really is; it is certainly one of the guitarist's best friends, and a technique that is unique to stringed instruments.

The key to improvisational success with this technique is to know the open notes available to you, and how they can apply to or work against the key you're playing in. For example, an open *G* would make an interesting 7th juxtaposition in the key of *A*, but you would probably avoid it like the plague in the key of *F#*! Obviously, lots of hammer-ons and pull-offs work well with this technique, but I prefer the more challenging, rapid alternate-picking approach for some wild effects.

To get started, Ex. 13 is one such lick in *G*, using the open *G* string over chromatically played fretted notes. Try to eventually play it as fast as possible.

Since the open *G* chord has those three nice open strings to work with, it would be nice to experiment with a lick that utilized the *B*, *G*, and *D* strings, like Ex. 14.

When you use an open note that is a bit more "outside" of the key you're in, such as open *G* in the key of *A*, you get some really interesting sounds. In Ex. 15 the *G* keeps driving home the lowered 7th of the key, even when most other licks would have given up.

The phrase can be lengthened, picking up on another open-string position later on down the line. In Ex. 16, we end up playing a descending run that utilizes the open *A*.

Finally we can combine the picking technique with hammers and pulls. Note that since we are using open strings, some of these hammer-ons can occur many frets up, creating a kind of "yodel" effect (Ex. 17).

These ideas have just scratched the surface, and I hope you try to find some new ones of your own within this technique. It never ceases to amaze me just how different each guitarist can sound and think, and I get excited at the very prospect of all the new and inventive things many of you must be coming up with.

Ex. 16

Ex. 17

Ex. 15

The two-note "claw" style

■ The two-note "claw" style is one of my favorite and most useful country guitar techniques. It probably got its name due to the funny, lobster-like, right-hand position employed by such artists as Jerry Reed and Chet Atkins. They both pick, or "claw," using their thumb and forefinger, but if you're not using a thumbpick, you may not get enough bite out of the lower string in each lick. For this reason, and because I'm very used to it, I prefer to use the flatpick-and-middle-finger approach. With this technique you can keep your picking very accurate and clean, and the rest of your picking hand can damp out the unwanted strings. If you already have a lot of calluses, it may not be necessary, but if you expect to match the

brightness of the flatpick, you should keep your nails long on the other fingers. It's good to find nice, tight, two-note positions that can be played in close proximity to each other.

Ex. 18 shows some warm-up positions, in both open and closed forms; note that the open position facilitates faster movement, while the closed offers some real challenges in left-hand preparedness and speed. This is especially apparent when going immediately from, say, a higher two-note lick to a two-string, Chuck Berry-like barre position many frets below it.

In Ex. 19, we see how the capabilities of this style can be extended to licks that use nonadjacent strings, such as

Ex. 18

the *E* and the *G,* or the *D* and the *B.* Again, I recommend trying the pick-and-middle-finger approach for these exercises. Play them slowly at first, making sure you're accurate in your moves from one set of double-stops to another. Be sure to keep your hand as close to the strings as possible, which helps you attack to the notes more cleanly while maintaining a good damping position.

Ex. 19

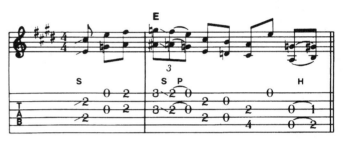

Constant bass licks

■ One of the great ways to build tension and intensity as a lead *or* rhythm player is the technique of juxtaposing a constant bass pattern against some licks or fills. Both right-hand techniques—either all flatpicking or the pick-and-fingers approach—work equally well, though the latter obviously allows you to hit every bass note, while the former forces you to sacrifice some of the bass notes when you need to pick the lead lines. The end result is almost the same, however, and the truly experienced flatpicker can execute these kinds of licks very well. It should be pointed out that, while this style is often associated with rhythm playing, it also applies to lead and can be put to good use in solos.

Ex. 20 is reminiscent of the playing of Pete Townshend, who so effectively uses the constant bass pattern over chords. This kind of piece should be played with all downstrokes, which add to the aggressive quality. Make

sure to let the picking hand leave the bass notes just enough to catch the chords on the beat.

It's also a pleasure to be able to catch certain higher, closed positions off this kind of lick. Ex. 21 is reminiscent of gospel or rockabilly; note how you can also use techniques such as hammer-ons in these licks with great results.

Perhaps the truest test of your accuracy within this style is when you can manage the constant bass while picking out single notes with the flatpick, as in Ex. 22. The addition of hammer-ons and pull-offs enable the left hand to play more notes, while the right hand can get back to the work of keeping the bass notes going. This homogenizing of the two parts is essential to creating a smooth technique, especially if you're flatpicking and want to approximate a fingerpicked-like effect.

Ex. 22 continued

Pick-and-finger arpeggios

■ This technique is associated with players such as Mark Knopfler, who incorporate both flatpicking and finger-picking in their electric guitar work. When I play in this style, I often abandon the pick altogether and simply fingerpick the whole lick. This approach gives you more control of damping and a more sensitive touch.

Basically, we are breaking up, or "rolling," a given chord formation, often adding additional higher notes. Go for a plucky, almost percussive picking sound, with each note ringing only for a very short time—the only sustained pitches should be the high notes at the ends of the phrases.

I had a chance to explore this style back in the '70s when I played with Tony Bird, a South African singer who turned me on to this style. You can also hear it in the work of the great Bahamian guitarist Joseph Spence, in calypso, and in just about any warm-climate guitar style. Anyway, it works great on electric, as you'll see in the licks in Ex. 23. Remember, there are two ways to play it: pick and two fingers, or thumb and three fingers. Take your "pick" and see what happens. Enjoy!

Ex. 23

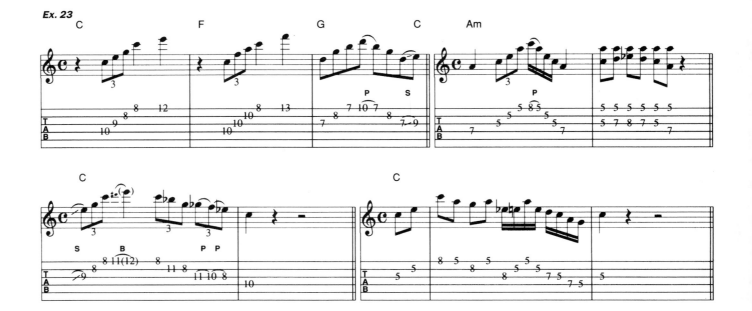

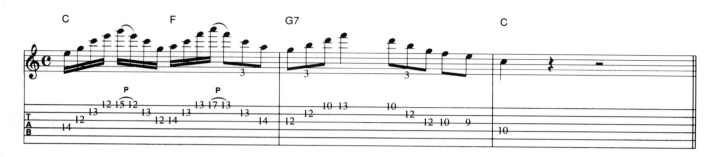

Using damped notes as part of a lick

■ Using damped notes as part of a phrase is one of the funkiest guitaristic "tricks." I've found that it adds a lot of character and personality whenever I use it. In country and blues playing, it can be likened to "chicken-pickin'" in its effect, especially when used with "false" [artificial] harmonics.

The best way to execute licks like these is to have the left hand follow directly over the notes you are damping. That way, even if you're not pressing down on the notes themselves, there is still a faint-sounding approximation of the note, plus you retain your hand position. Of course, this technique lends itself most readily to flat-picking.

For Ex. 24, I recommend digging in a bit with the notes on the *G* string while trying to create a stinging, "false" harmonic tone on the high *E* string. Use strict alternate picking. Ex. 25 calls for a B.B. King-style blues approach. The damped arpeggio notes fly by very quickly, with only the top notes truly sounding. The contrast between the damped notes and the sustained notes with vibrato gives us the "sting" we want—you hear this a lot in B.B.'s playing. Be sure to play this lick in one straight downward picking motion.

Ex. 24

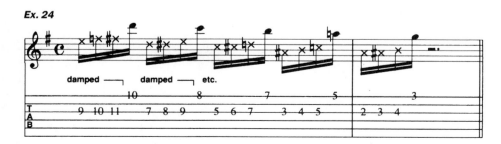

Ex. 26, one of my old favorites, is a blues or jazz guitarist's way of simulating a well-known piano riff. (But with the damping, it's purely guitar—and that's what we're after, right?) For the damping, lay your pinky across the middle four strings at the 7th fret, damping the first three, but fretting the note on the fifth string.

Ex. 27 uses damping to create a descending pattern of three-note arpeggiated chords. Play them with fairly aggressive downstrokes, carefully fretting the last note of each chord. In Ex. 28, the damped notes lead up to a high bent note. I've added a few more notes so you can see how the technique might be used as part of a longer lick.

Ex. 25

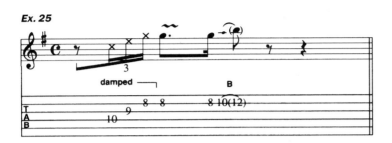

Ex. 26

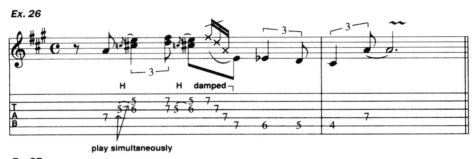

Ex. 27

Ex. 28

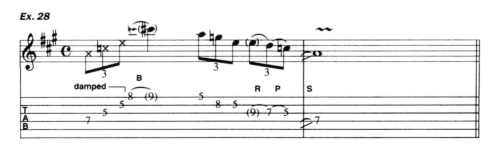

The mini barre

■ Small, partial barres serve a different purpose than those big ones you slap across your strings. The little guys are good for smoothing transitions within a run or scale; they demand more finesse than strength. Let's see how mini barres can supercharge your licks.

One important mini barre is a rapid dual-string grip that moves quickly across the neck. This is handy for playing scales that lie within a very close "box" area, such as those in Ex. 29 and 30. Using mini barres, hammer-ons, and pull-offs, you can extract some tasty licks from these patterns.

To get a feel for this, try Ex. 31. In measure 1, barre the first and second strings at the 3rd fret. Shift string sets twice within bar 2 (barre the second and third strings for beats one and two; third and fourth strings, beats three and four).

Ex. 32 carries the mini barre even farther across the fretboard. In measure 1, barre the first and second strings at the 5th fret. In each subsequent measure, move the barre across the neck one string set (second and third strings, bar 2; third and fourth strings, bar 3; fourth and fifth strings, bar 4).

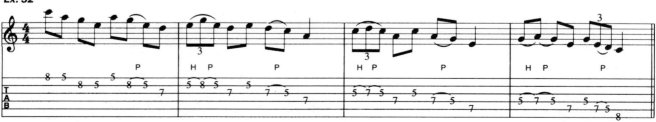

In Ex. 33, the partial barres shift position more dramatically. This example begins with a major pentatonic country position, mutates into a jazzier dominant 9th sound, and then closes with a Nashville twang.

Experiment with mini barres on your own, and try to work them into improvisations. Onward!

Ex. 33

Open-position "roll" licks

■ As an interesting variation on the same old shuffles and open-position licks one is called on to play as a guitarist, I've come up with some open-position "roll" licks. I call them this because they are best played with a pick-and-fingers approach, using a hammer-on and barre-position combination that lends itself to the "roll" sound. For those familiar with my recordings, this style is best exemplified on my song "Restless Age," from the *Hot Pickups* album [Rounder].

For the pick-and-fingers approach, use the flatpick and both the middle and ring fingers for the following exercises. The pick is involved only on the lowest string of each lick, and then the other fingers follow the remaining strings in natural order. It's important when assuming the "ready" position for these licks that the pick and fingers be already positioned on the strings themselves. This not only helps you achieve the roll sound properly, it enables you to damp the strings until they are needed. This way, we can move this three-stringed grouping conveniently from one chord to another in a sort of "block" formation.

Left-hand partial barres are necessary and helpful, since you can place many hammer-ons and pull-offs directly over them; just be sure to press them down firmly enough to make them sustain well. If you can put all of these techniques together successfully into one

package, you should be able to tackle this style with ease. If not, then one little hitch in the system could make things difficult for you. In any event, let's try Ex. 34 in the open position of *E*. Have your pick and fingers in the ready position before you start, and be sure to play all of the hammers and pulls as indicated.

Ex. 34

Ex. 35

In Ex. 35 we have variations on the standard roll pattern. In this case, we are using pull-offs and the open *D* string to change things around. My favorite open position for roll licks is *A*. Here we can literally duplicate what we were doing for *E*, moved up one string to the *A*, *D*, and *G* strings. Ex. 36 shows the standard position and the newer variations all rolled into one.

The position for *D* (Ex. 37) doesn't contain a partial barre, but it is no more difficult to execute than the *E* or *A* positions. The only real trick lies in using the 2nd finger as part of the initial hammer-on on the *D* string, just before it crosses over to be used on the *B* string.

Finally, in Ex. 38 we have the same type of roll for open *G*, played on the high three strings. Since a more radical shift in position is required, we'll use a *slide* with our 2nd finger on the *G* string to simulate what the hammer-ons were doing in the previous examples. Try to incorporate these exercises into your own ideas, and by all means have fun!

Open-string pull-offs & hammer-ons

■ One flashy technique you can occasionally use is open-string hammer-on and pull-off licks (Ex. 39). These are particularly effective when the lick follows a phrase played higher on the neck, above normal open-position pull-off territory.

The key to creating and understanding these licks is to know the musical value of the open strings while you're riffing in the higher positions. It's important to learn how each key has its own particular relationships to the open strings, since they have very different meanings in, say, the keys of *C* and *F#*. The *E* and *G* strings are actually part of the *C* chord; in *F#*, the open strings may not be part of the basic chords, but they can still work as single-note lines.

But most of all, this technique is just plain fun, and it's one of the easiest to experiment with. Even if one of your ideas falls flat on its face, it can still make some sort of

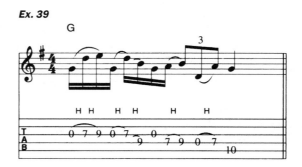

→

Ex. 39 continued

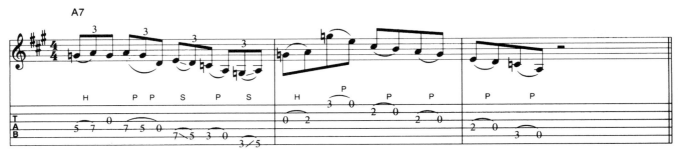

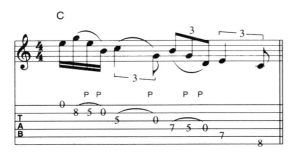

sense. Many "mistakes" become pleasant surprises, giving birth to new licks that would have been impossible in any "normal" positions. And remember—these licks are *supposed* to sound different.

The key to enjoying the true potential of this style is to experiment as much as you can! So go for it—you just may surprise yourself. Happy hunting!

Slick Turnarounds and Cool Licks

Twenty years of guitar licks

■ *Guitar Player* magazine marked its 20th anniversary a number of years ago, and in celebration I wrote out some of my favorite licks, old and new (Ex. 1). When *Guitar Player* started, I was a cocky guitar-slinging kid who was honing his skills while fronting a Bronx-based band. I was on the threshold of developing a true understanding of lead guitar, as the blues boom was about to hit me when I went to high school. But these were still days of playing early Stones and Beatles material, along with my original songs.

I find that a lot of kids today are learning the same licks that were important then. It seems that the "20-year-recycling" is happening with musical trends as well as everything else, and the music of the mid and late "60s is enjoying a real comeback. There was a lot of experimenting going on in the '60s, in a free and innocent atmosphere. Sure, today's kids are given much more exposure to various forms of music and education—witness a magazine like *Guitar Player*, for example—but, of course, there's so much more *to* know these days! Today, you'll find a 12-year-old who may decide to bypass a 1965 Byrds lick and go directly to Yngwie Malmsteen instead. This is all fine, but I hope that many of these aspiring guitarists remember to go to the *source* and not take today as square one.

When I toured Japan a few years ago, I needed a different back-up band in each city. Since my set was simple, and I made sure to include lots of I, IV, V-type progressions, I thought there would be few problems—a simple run-through with the band before each show should suffice. Well, I was in for the shock of my life when I found that some young players who could handle the most difficult fusion and jazz had never played a simple *blues!* It seemed that they had their heroes, and that's who they learned to play from, by rote. Needless to say, their playing lacked a lot of soul, and it was one of the tougher (and more bizarre) sets I'd ever had to play.

When I toured with Duane Eddy in 1986, we opened for Huey Lewis & The News on a mammoth tour, and it was incredible to see how well-received we were, considering that we were opening for the act with the #1 record in the country and that we were all-instrumental and playing music that was 25 years old! It just shows that what once was cool can be cool again, not to mention that Huey's audiences appeared to be as sweet and classy as he and his band are. No high-tech there, just good old rock and roll played for people who want to have a good time. That's what it will *always* be about!

Use these licks well and make them and all your playing count in the years to come.

➤

Ex. 1

play simultaneously

play simultaneously

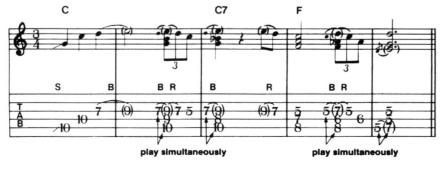

play simultaneously   play simultaneously

Southern rock harmonies for one

The sound of so-called "Southern Rock" has long been associated with double-guitar harmony parts. This was pioneered and best exemplified by Duane Allman and Dickey Betts of the original Allman Brothers Band. It then went on to become part of the sound of countless other Southern rockers, such as the Marshall Tucker Band, Lynyrd Skynyrd, and also in the country rock of Charlie Daniels, Alabama, and Hank Williams, Jr. This double-guitar sound eventually reached places such as New York and L.A., as you can hear in Elliot Randall's solo on Steely Dan's "Reeling In The Years" [*Steely Dan— Greatest Hits,* MCA] and on the guitar break in just about any lush big-production-type ballad of the '70s.

I have always been intrigued with the prospect and challenge of creating these kinds of parts with one guitar.

Generally speaking, many of the well-known harmony solos began freely, like any other solo, then eventually built into a repeating pattern before finally becoming harmonized as the second part entered. It should also be noted that this technique can be used to great effect for unison playing and octaves, as well as harmonies.

In the solo in Ex. 2, I've recreated a typical way in which one of these harmony solos can be developed. The only difference is that you're actually playing the two parts by yourself. This requires some very accurate fingering in tight spaces, and it can get a little crowded. So be careful, and take it slow at first—especially when it comes to the hammer-ons and pull-offs. Good luck with it!

Block chords in lead work

■ The use of "block" chords in lead playing has been popularized by players such as Mark Knopfler, Amos Garrett, and others. It's a direct result of the pick-and-finger technique you've heard me talk about so much.

This particular style of picking opens up lots of possibilities: rolling the chord's notes, hammering-on and pulling-off with better control, blocking, damping, and more. What's also nice is that you can weave in and out of rhythm and lead styles without changing positions.

I used this technique a lot at the point in my career when I was accompanying solo artists such as Eric Andersen, Tony Bird, John Prine, and Steve Goodman. They needed me to fill out their sound, so the block chord/lead guitar approach was a natural, both on acoustic and electric. I've used it on solo efforts such as "When A Man Loves A Woman" and "Unchained Melody," playing the melody within the three-note chord.

Before we get on with the examples, there's one more trick you should know: When playing melodies such as these, you can use vibrato to accent an individual note within the chord, making it act as the "lead singer" while the other two notes essentially "sing" a supporting harmony. This helps the melody stand out and makes the whole lick more interesting. This works best on the highest string of the lick, with the vibrato created by a subtle pull and release of the index finger.

The examples of the style in Ex. 3 should all be played with the pick and two fingers. Keep it melodic-sounding, and you'll be in business.

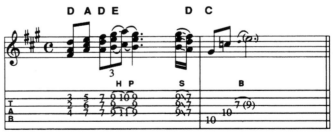

Using open strings for speed

■ Using open strings can make runs move more quickly and sound more interesting. I've found open strings to be most at home in country, rockabilly, and blues styles, but you can also apply them to rock and even metal. Not only are they great for that twangy sound, but they also help immensely in pulling off whole groups of notes. Some of the examples in Ex. 4 combine the open strings with higher positions, as opposed to staying in the neighboring lower positions. Hopefully, this idea will spawn more experimentation on your part.

As guitarists, we're drawn to keys such as *E*, *A*, *D*, and *G*, which allow us to use many open notes. The guitar is just built that way, and to my ear those keys sound best. Furthermore, the open positions offer many creative possibilities, while still affording all the closed positions. But there is a distinct difference between the sound of a picked open string and the sound of an open string as part of a hammer-on or pull-off lick. Open strings are quite a bit looser than fretted ones, so tread lightly when flatpicking your notes!

I've selected a few licks in various keys to show you just some of each key's potential (Ex. 4). Try making up some of your own—believe me, we've only scratched the surface.

Ex. 4

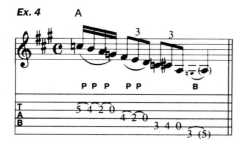

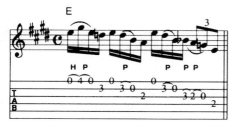

Ex. 4 continued

Slick turnarounds & other coolness

■ The licks in Ex. 5 are in a blues and country bag, but you can certainly adapt them to fit jazz or rock styles as well. It's healthy to experiment with anything you learn.

As usual, I recommend the pick-and-finger approach to playing these licks. Why? You'll get better damping, blocking, and an overall cleaner attack.

Here's a tip: When a run starts with two strings and works its way down toward the low *E* string, start with your pick and middle finger. Lead with the middle finger as the lick continues. In this manner, you are always working in groups of two strings at a time, using the pick and middle finger. If a third, higher string is involved, you can use the ring finger without having to shift right-hand position.

If you want to wail with pick and fingers, it's important to teach your right hand to quickly and instinctively assume what I call the "ready" position. It works like this: Your pick, middle, and ring fingers "grab" or rest on the three top strings. The fleshy part of the hand below the thumb rests across the remaining lower strings. This technique is indispensable for proper damping; it lets you create a clean tone without accidentally sounding unwanted notes.

➤

Ex. 5

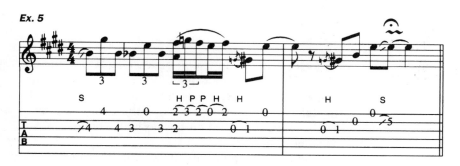

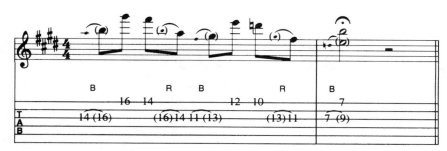

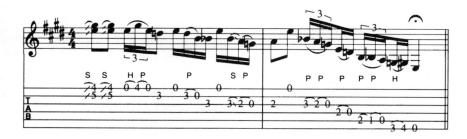

Boxes of knowledge

■ Self-taught players love discovering fingerboard areas that can be milked for all they're worth! I'd always played by ear and feel and never thought of "box" positions except in an abstract sense. That all changed when I wrote my first book, *Slide Guitar,* and was required to locate areas where licks could be created within a small area.

The most commonly taught box position produces a pentatonic run across all six strings. I refer to this as the "B.B. King box," the high pentatonic position that gives birth to so many of B.B.'s trademark licks. Now I'd like to shed light on some less-used positions that can be fruitful sources for improvisational ideas.

Ex. 6, based on a dominant chord shape that looks like a first-position *A7,* produces a jazzy sound that can be used in a blues context. Ex. 7 illustrates some possibilities. Come up with some of your own ideas.

Ex. 8 involves quite a bit of reaching. Study the diagram and the notation—you'll see that the resulting major pentatonic scale is formed around the shape of a typical barre chord with its root on the sixth string. Ex. 9, an extended run based on this position, should give you some new ideas.

Hammer-ons, pull-offs, slides, and other devices can turn a box position into a fountain of knowledge. Be sure to apply your own phrasing ideas. Also, look for more box positions on the fingerboard—they're endless!

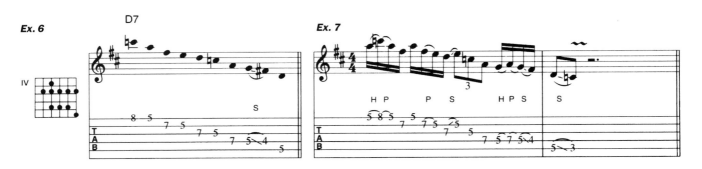

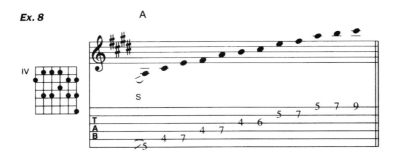

Hot licks down under, mate!

■ Lots of new teaching ideas crop up whenever I give clinics, and my tour of Australia a few years ago was no exception. A lot of students "down under" had questions about my pick-and-finger style (particularly in open positions) and my various harmonic and "false" harmonic tricks. Ex.10 shows some of the open-position pick-and-finger licks that I use a lot. Most of them use the middle finger in conjunction with the pick; I feel that this combination affords the most strength and speed. The right-hand fingerings are indicated; "p" represents the pick, "m", the middle finger, and "a", the ring finger.

I do a type of "chicken pickin'" that incorporates a "false" harmonic, a *backstroke* harmonic that's created by striking the string with the thumb and *then* catching the string with the pick, to produce the harmonic. (Most of my "false" harmonics use the more traditional downstroke approach, whereby the thumb produces the harmonic *after* the pick strikes the string.) The harmonics in Ex.11 should be played as "backstroke" harmonics. The Ex.11 licks are played with the flatpick only.

Ex. 10

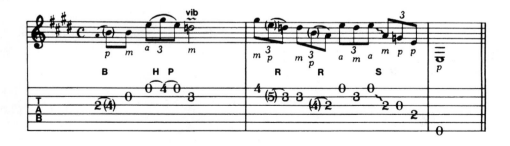

Ex. 11

Ten years of Hot Guitar

■ In ten years of writing the Hot Guitar column for *Guitar Player,* I received many letters from readers. Those letters never failed to give me new ideas and concepts, and keep me in touch with what the readers wanted. To celebrate my tenth anniversary of writing the column, I came up with some of my favorite licks.

The licks in Ex. 12 cover lots of stylistic ground—rock, country, rockabilly, blues. Integrate their ideas into your own bag of tricks and feel free to change them to your heart's content.

Ex. 12

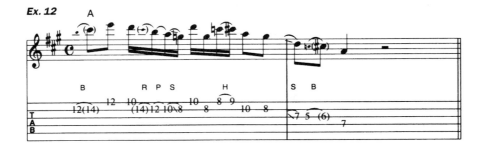

Ex. 13   A

Ex. 14   G

Ex. 15   G   **Ex. 16**   E

Rapid-Fire Rockabilly

Some rockabilly flash

■ Being a rockabilly fanatic, I thought I'd shed some light on this not-talked-about-enough subject. The name "rockabilly" tells the story of the style's origins: rock and roll, mixed with "hillbilly," or country playing. An important ingredient of the rockabilly sound was Merle Travis' "Travis picking" technique, which enabled guitarists to fingerpick a melody on the high strings while keeping a steady bass part with the thumb. (Ike Everly, the Everly Brothers' father, also contributed to the development of this technique.) Some rockabilly players use a thumbpick, while others favor the flat-pick-and-finger approach. I prefer the latter because it enables you to go into straight flatpicking at any time. For rockabilly at its best, listen to Scotty Moore (with Elvis Presley), the great Carl Perkins, and the wild, wonderful Cliff Gallup (with Gene Vincent's Bluecaps).

Ex. 1 is what I call a "harmony shuffle" lick—it's real cool and *very* rockabilly. The flatpick plays the lower notes, while the middle finger covers the high ones. In Ex. 2, the constant bass creates a bottom that supports an independent lead part. Go for total separation; this technique works best when it sounds like two guitars are playing. Ex. 3, with its alternating bass line, shows the Travis influence. Some of the lead notes are conveniently played in unison with the bass notes, while others are sort of slipped into the alternating pattern, heightening the two-guitar effect.

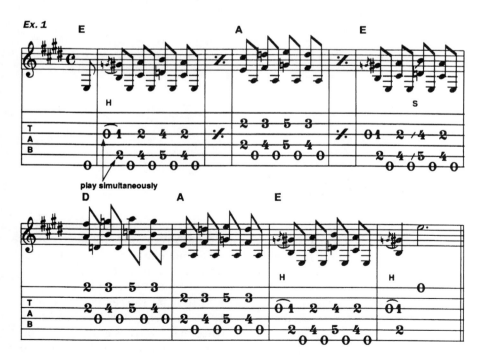

Ex. 1

Ex. 2

Rockabilly with a constant bass

■ The rockabilly sound fascinates many guitarists, myself included. When I first heard the style, I was immediately drawn to the constant-bass sound.

Although the style originated among fingerpickers like Merle Travis, Ike Everly, Chet Atkins, and Joe Maphis, current players such as Danny Gatton, ,Eric Johnson, and I use the pick-and-finger method. Although you sacrifice the use of your right-hand index finger, your damping ability is increased, plus you can always go back to straight flatpicking.

I think the toughest aspect of this style is maintaining the separation between the bass and lead notes. A good way to achieve this independence is to practice parts in which the lead figures relate well to the bass patterns. For example, try playing a shuffle eighth-note feel in the bass against a triplet pattern on top, as in Ex. 4. This three-notes-for-two situation helps "lock" your picking hand into a groove. Once that groove is established, you can take chances and go off on more exploratory lead ventures.

Another popular approach uses straight eighth-notes in the bass, as in Ex. 5. Left-hand techniques such as slides, hammers, and pull-offs all lend character and independence to the lead part.

Start both exercises with just the bass lines, and then lay the lead parts over them once they feel locked in.

Rockabilly bass patterns

■ When I play country or rockabilly on electric, I inevitably slip into the alternating-bass "Travis picking" style. Merle Travis and most other players associated with the style use their thumb to play the bass notes, but as I've mentioned, I prefer to use the flatpick, with my middle and ring fingers sounding the lead notes on top.

The advantage of this method is that you can switch from straight flatpicking to fingerpicking in the blink of an eye, and the flatpick gives the bass notes a good "edge." The disadvantage is that you lose the use of the index finger, which must grip the pick. Some traditional players get around this by using a thumbpick for the bass notes, freeing three fingers for the lead parts. But when they have to break into a single note line without a bass part, the thumbpick must play part of the lead run. Now I don't know about you, but I have a hard time grasping the concept of using my thumb to play lead! That's why my style is the direct outgrowth of being a *lead* player,

someone who needs to switch from technique to technique with a minimum of effort.

Ex. 6 shows how the open strings help you play licks over *E* and *A* chords and how you can incorporate hammer-ons in the lead part. Notice that the 2nd finger of your fretting hand must alternate between the fifth and sixth strings when you get to the *B7* chord. This is a classic Travis-type lick, so it would be good to get it down.

We take it up the neck a bit for Ex. 7. Even though we're working in a more closed position, we still rely on the open fifth string. Note that many of the lead notes are pinched simultaneously with a bass note.

Ex. 8 shows the possibilities—and limitations—of working in a totally closed position—in this case, the key of *G*. We must maintain a complete barre chord across all six strings while slipping in some notes on top of the bass line. This one may be a little uncomfortable at first, so take your time with it.

Rapid-fire patterns

■ Pickers like Danny Gatton, Albert Lee, and myself have been promoting the wonderful style of rockabilly for quite some time. The words "hot licks" truly apply to rockabilly playing, as anyone who's listened to the style can attest.

Rockabilly guitar involves a rapid succession of notes played with a country/blues flavor. I don't use the straight "picking every note" approach as much as some of my peers do, but I often combine pick and fingers to create fast "roll" licks and other rapid-fire patterns.

Another helpful trick is the use of chromatic patterns that fall easily within the reach of your fingers. These allow you to play fast runs, and they afford the option of using hammer-ons and pull-offs instead of picking every note. They also let you move from one position to another with a minimum of time lost.

Try playing the patterns in Ex. 9 with the flatpick alone and with flatpick and fingers together. The two sounds are definitely different, but you should try to attain the same speed with both techniques.

Ex. 9

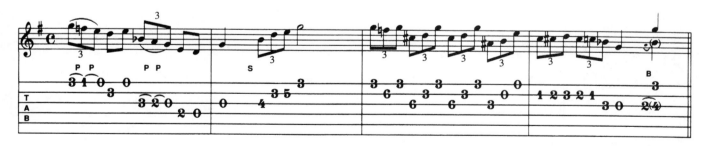

Banjo-style rolls

■ When I do clinics, people always ask me how they can develop more independence for pick-and-finger playing. I always end up using certain open-position "roll" licks in *G* to illustrate the sort of patterns that can help develop that independence.

These licks can really be fun and rewarding, especially when you get them up to speed and play them in a rapid-fire rockabilly style. The key is to go for the bright, almost mechanical sound of a banjo or steel guitar. And speaking of steel guitar, this technique also helps in recreating *that* sound, as well—you'll notice I've thrown in a few steel guitar-style bends to illustrate this.

In Ex. 10, we get into the groove with a simple, repetitious pattern that involves the pick and two fingers, along with a hammer-on. Next, the dissonant "banjo" roll sets in, emphasizing a repeated three-note figure. Ex. 11 is quite similar, but it includes some of those "pedal-steel" bends. And just think—we're still playing *guitar* here!

Ex. 12 is played in closed position. It still sounds country, but it's in the basic blues position that we all know so well (I hope). As in Ex. 11, you'll need to support the bend with extra fingers while trying to maintain the pitch of the top two notes—no easy task!

Ex. 10

Ex. 11

Ex. 12

Open-string rockabilly twangin'

■ One cool way to spice up your playing is to throw a few open strings into your licks. Yeah, I've touched on this technique before, but this time we're going to look at some new applications.

Adding an open string to a lick can create the illusion that the position is being stretched. This is analogous to the way metal players use tapping to extend the range of their licks. Open strings generate different musical effects, according to the key you're playing in.

The trio of licks in Ex. 13 to 15 are in the key of *G*. The three open strings in a *G* triad impart a very clean, "yodeling" quality—no dissonance here. Play Ex. 13 with a swing feel, and let the open strings ring throughout.

In Ex. 16 and 17 we move up to the key of *A*. Instantly, some of the open strings take on a twangier character. Notice how the notes in both licks seem to weave around the open *G*—it adds a dominant 7th sound.

Applying open strings to licks in *D* produces yet another effect. Here, the open *G* and *B* strings imply a gospel-like IV chord suspended against the *D* riffs—check out the harmonies in Ex. 18.

Although I think of such open-string licks as coming from rockabilly, you can apply the technique to practically any style. See if you can discover new ways to incorporate open strings in your favorite licks.

Ex. 13

Ex. 14

Ex. 15

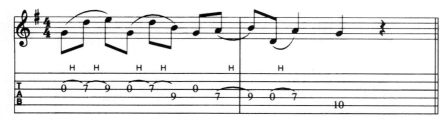

Ex. 16

Ex. 17

Ex. 18

Rockabilly ruckus

■ You know rockabilly guitar is near and dear to my heart—and yours too, I trust. Let's tackle some hot arpeggiated runs and chord-like riffs that work well with this style.

The licks in Ex. 19 should be played relatively fast with plenty of attack. The chord licks are based on big band horn section-like riffs. The double-stop runs can be played with a flatpick alone, but for accuracy and clarity I recommend the pick-and-fingers approach.

To reinforce your rockabilly feel, listen to Brian Setzer, Cliff Gallup (with Gene Vincent & The Blue Caps), Danny Gatton, Albert Lee, and James Burton. This style broke a lot of rules when it first showed up, so feel free to break a few of your own.

Ex. 19

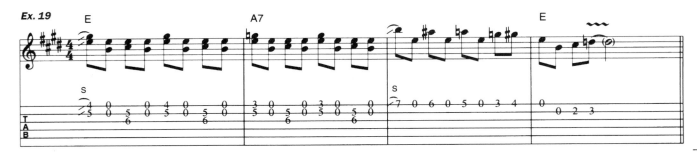

Ex. 19 continued

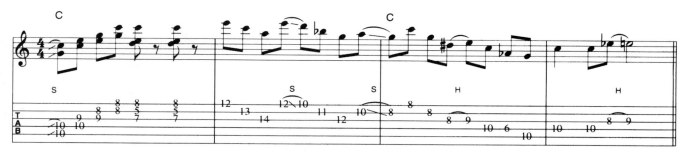

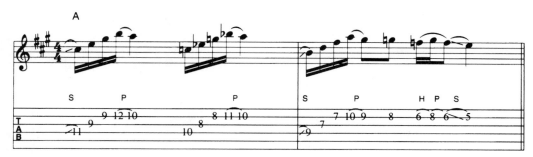

Blues Power

"Butterfly" vibrato

■ For several years now people have been paying more attention to blues and blues guitar playing. When the *first* major blues "rediscovery" took place around 1966, I was inspired by players such as Mike Bloomfield, B.B. King, Buddy Guy, and Otis Rush. And with folks like Eric Clapton and Albert King still going strong, there's an incredible wealth of blues material to choose from.

Although many play the blues, few approach blues guitar in the proper manner. I know that sounds too scholarly (like saying there's only one way to paint a picture), but certain techniques enable you to get maximum expression out of the blues, and expression is what it's all about, isn't it?

Take vibrato, for example. It's one of the most crucial "vocal" elements of blues guitar, but I've seen players with 15 years' experience who don't know how to get the proper vibrato sound. This is usually due to lack of strength and a failure to understand what I call the B.B. King "butterfly" vibrato style, in which you pivot your entire hand, off the side of the neck, as shown in the photo.

Notice that the string is slightly bent. That's because the vibrato sound should result from a continuous bending and releasing of the string. Don't concentrate too much on the fretted note itself; just let the vibrato be a by-product of the total motion of your hand.

When you play this 12-bar solo in Ex.1, emphasize the "traditional" aspects of blues soloing and phrasing. Don't forget to emphasize the vocal quality of the music with vibrato and bends. Always commit your *entire* hand to these techniques—it will really pay off in the long run.

Ex. 1

➡

Ex. 1 continued

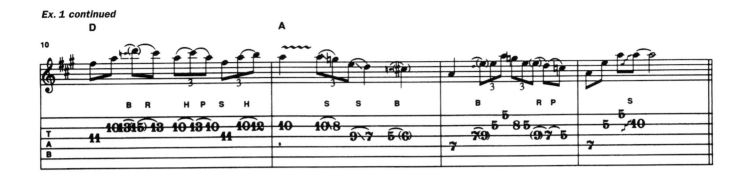

"Question-and-answer" phrasing

■ The blues is based on a "question-and-answer" type of phrasing. Also it's crucial to keep in mind that from the moment the very first note or phrase is played, you're committed to the overall balance of the entire solo. It's like telling a joke or story; if the rhythm and continuity are interrupted, you've lost the listener's interest.

You don't need to know every lick and scale in the world to create an effective blues solo. All you need is a few notes, an ear, and a sense of purpose to what you are saying with your instrument. Listen to players such as B.B. King, Buddy Guy, and Otis Rush; each has a distinctive, "trademark" sound, yet each can improvise freely and completely within it, regardless of the circumstances.

The melody and phrasing of the solo in Ex. 2 have a decidedly B.B. King-style flavor. Note the solo's "up" feeling, due largely to the use of major pentatonic (root, 2, 3, 5, 6) positions. Also, notice how much we can say in just 12 bars, using a small area of the fingerboard.

Ex. 2

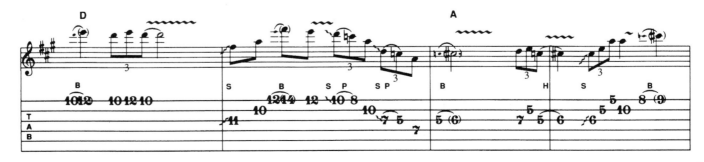

Ex. 2 continued

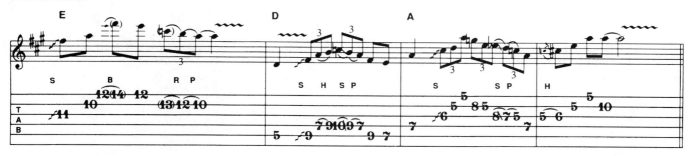

Rooted in the blues: Eric Clapton

■ While borrowing from a variety of influences, Eric Clapton always has maintained a high quality in his music. A player with deep blues roots, he manages to integrate facets of B.B. King's and Otis Rush's styles with his own highly personal approach. Regardless of the type of song he's playing, it's easy to recognize his sound. Eric's classic, unique vibrato, bending style, and phrasing are three elements that enabled him to produce some of rock guitar's most memorable lines.

The key to Clapton's vibrato (and most great rock vibratos) is left-hand *pivoting* motion. Pivoting is crucial because it enables you to vibrato as slow or as fast as you desire, giving you complete control. The first two photos show a before/after perspective of an index-finger vibrato *a la* B.B. King, where the pivot rocks the hand so that it contacts the side of the fingerboard. When playing this type of vibrato, it is the pivot itself that makes the tip of the finger move the string. So it's the motion of the whole hand to keep in mind, rather than sending all of your energy to the tip of your finger. Note that when the pivot is in its full downward motion, your hand directly faces the guitar.

While Clapton's string-bending approach is much imitated, few have managed to produce his degree of emotion. The key is not only his sweeping bending sound but also his use of vibrato in tandem with some of his more extreme bends. When bending away from you, vibrato is not so hard to attain, because pivoting motion can be applied to both the vibrato and the bend (see third photo).

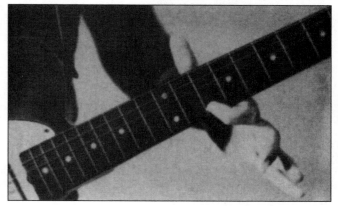

➤

On the other hand, when you bend *towards* you (see last photo), the vibrato comes from exercising complete control over a bend/release motion to create the wavering effect. It doesn't sound too difficult, but maintaining an even pulsation and pitch is something that will take a lot of practice until you build up your hand strength.

Clapton's phrasing and feeling are two of his most important stylistic elements. In the six licks shown in Ex.3, I've tried to capture some of this for you. In the case of phrases that use notes at the same fret on adjacent strings, such as the 7th fret on the *G* and *D* strings, try to use a rapid 3rd-finger barre. This is a technique that Eric often employs, and it helps distinguish his blues licks from those of other players. For the most part, I recommend that you mainly use a three-finger left-hand approach. Your vibrato will be better because your third finger is quite a bit stronger than your pinky (resort to your pinky only if you can't reach a particular stretch). Good luck and keep that slowhand slow! Note: In the first half of the first beat in the final lick (and all similar phrases), pluck the two 12s simultaneously, quickly bending to the 14.

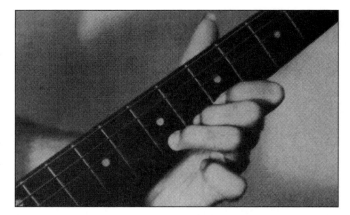

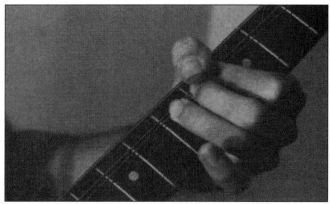

Ex. 3

Blues licks in the open position

■ When you hear the playing of such greats as John Fogerty, Carl Perkins, Mark Knopfler, and Steve Cropper, it's sometimes the licks containing open strings that hit home the most. Sure, these guys can get around the neck just fine, but there is a certain meatiness that can be achieved by working the lower positions. Fogerty, in particular, uses these licks as hooks or signatures. Just take a listen to "The Old Man Down The Road" [*Centerfield*, Warner Bros.] or Credence Clearwater's "Green River" [*Green River*, Fantasy] to see what I mean. This type of playing has its roots way back in Delta blues, but it's as important and emotional today as it was when Robert Johnson, Son

House, and Lightnin' Hopkins first fooled around with it. I like to take some of my flashier solos down to the lower frets to make a different statement, especially when I'm in the benevolent keys of *E, A, D,* or *G*. This is obviously because these particular keys contain open strings, and there are blues patterns that exist for them on the lowest frets. Ex. 4 shows some of the patterns I like to work within.

Some very handy licks can be created with the combination of fretted notes and open strings, and you can really get a lot of creative mileage out of them. A few are shown in Ex. 5.

When coming up with licks for the key of *A*, a whole new flavor can be achieved. We do share common open notes with the *E* positions, such as an open 7th, 4th, and root (Ex. 6).

The key of *G* also has an open position that, like *E*, allows for the combination of fretted runs with open strings. There are also some really wonderful licks that can be created with bends in harmony with some of the open strings. I recommend a pick-and-fingers approach for these (Ex. 7).

Last, in Ex. 8, we have the open position for *D*, which requires some of the more unusual fingerings to create these kinds of runs. Take note especially of the lick that uses the bend on the low *E* string, and then resolves to the higher, open *D*.

Ex. 7

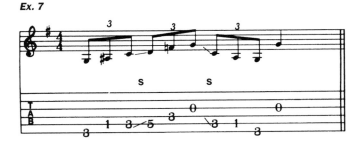

Ex. 8

Ex. 6

Rooted in the blues: John Fogerty

■ John Fogerty has always been, and will always remain, one of my all-time heroes. Few artists have been able to take the guitar, so simply and purely, and make it the center of great songs and grooves the way John does. A technical wiz he isn't, and thank God for that! He can make an old lick new, and a new lick a classic, all with the true essence of rock and roll and rhythm and blues.

We can certainly thank Fogerty for creating some of the most memorable, singable guitar parts of the last 15 years, and whether he was copying the solo of Roy Orbison's "Ooby Dooby" note for note [*Cosmo's Factory*, Fantasy] or creating his own to a song such as "Bad Moon Rising" [*Green River*, Fantasy], he played them all with equal love and real emotion.

→

John draws his influence from some of the purest blues and rockabilly roots, which is obvious from all of the early classics that he covered on his albums with Creedence Clearwater Revival (e.g., Dale Hawkins' "Susie Q," Little Richard's "Good Golly Miss Molly," Screamin' Jay Hawkins' "I Put A Spell On You," among others). Yet he was able to employ these techniques in his own songs with equal finesse and trueness to form. In fact, if you listen to most of his songs, past and present, you'll note his subtle use of montages of these types of guitar sounds to masterful effect. Often superimposing dirty sounds against clean, he would create memorable and distinctive dialogs between two, and sometimes three, guitars.

John's classic hit "Green River" has always epitomized the soul of his playing to me, and made great use of his overdubbing montage technique. Ex. 9 shows some of the open-position blues licks he used in this and many other great songs. Keep in mind that these were often played on a very clean, loosely strung guitar that gave them an added twang and a certain punch that was perfect for the licks. Note the use of bends, sometimes bent up first, then gradually let down through the passing tones, creating that nasty John Fogerty effect.

John also makes use of many great traditional double-note positions in combination with bends, as seen in Ex. 10. Some of these are related to early country blues styles, others to the later Chicago blues and Chuck Berry styles. Remember that you should use as many fingers as are available *behind* the bent note for added strength. This especially applies to bends of more than a half-step.

Ex. 9

Ex. 10

Standing at the crossroads

■ When Columbia Pictures called me in 1985, I immediately knew I was in store for one of my more unusual gigs. A guitar instructor was needed for *Crossroads*, a film involving a young classical guitarist who falls in love with the blues and wants to follow the legend of Robert Johnson. This meant I had to teach actor Ralph Macchio to play classical, slide, fingerpicking, and electric lead guitar—at least well enough so that he could fake the parts. Ry Cooder oversaw and composed the film's main soundtrack.

Ralph, who had previously starred in *The Karate Kid*, had never held a guitar before, but at the first lesson I realized that he was to be no ordinary student. I've never seen anyone absorb the guitar quite like him. Before going on location, we met for two hours a day, four to five days a week, for two-and-a-half months. Originally, we were hoping that Ralph could actually play some of the parts in the film, but as time passed, it was decided that I would play most of his parts, while he faked to the tracks.

His hands being small, the reaches required in classical playing were especially difficult. We went to see Segovia in concert, but that didn't shed much light on technique—Segovia seems so loose and relaxed. Director Arthur Hill wanted rigid, intense, two-dimensional classical music; of course, Ralph just wanted to get up and rock! I started him out on a simple but steady diet of classical arpeggios (Ex. 11), and some lead and slide sale positions (Ex. 12 and 13, respectively). We discovered that, while it may be one of the most difficult styles to play, slide guitar is definitely the easiest to visually fake. As long as the slide was moving in the right direction of the lick, generally, and the right hand looked okay, we were safe. Plus, Ralph was getting pretty damn good at it.

He had heard my piece "Landslide" [*Arlen Roth/Guitarist*, Rounder], and wanted to learn it (Ex. 14). For the scene where the character reaches the "crossroads," I re-recorded the song at 5:45 AM in the muddy field where he was to stand—without question, my weirdest recording date ever! I must admit, though, it was quite a thrill to hear my slide playing fading into the Mississippi morning, with no other sound but some crappies jumping in the nearby swamps.

So that Ralph would appear totally convincing, we spent hours making each beat of a B. B. King-style vibrato

Ex. 12

Ex. 11

even, bending strings just the right distance, and learning which notes should be picked when. I videotaped him, played it back, and critiqued his style. We also stood facing each other, and I played the part while he concentrated only on faking it.

When the crew was working on a scene not involving

guitar, I had some time to scout pawnshops and jam in local clubs with harmonica player Frank Frost. In fact, Frank ended up being flown to Hollywood to shoot a barroom scene. When he walked onto the Hollywood set for the first time, Frost simply strolled up to the bar and ordered a Bud. Guess the set designers were pretty accurate!

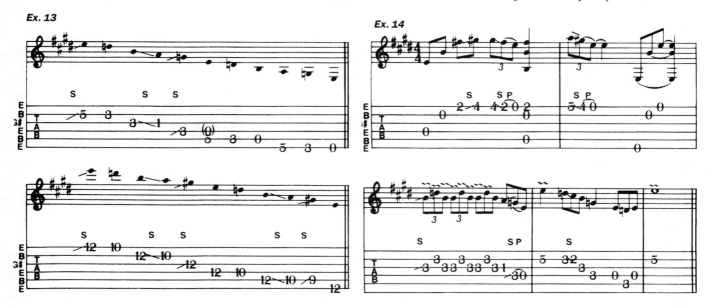

Ex. 13

Ex. 14

Single-note major blues bends

■ Over the years I've noticed that when a player gets into string-bending, particularly in the blues idiom, he often overlooks the *major* single-note bends that can greatly add to the versatility of a blues sound. Unfortunately, not everybody has the greatest ear, and as a consequence a lot of players get bogged down in a *minor*-only way of playing, even within a major blues context. It's true that many refer to these minor notes as "blue" notes, but I feel that the true blue notes are the ones that exist between the minor and major thirds, and between, say, the fourth and the fifth. These notes are most easily achieved by bending, a technique that is, of course, closely associated with the blues.

Perhaps the most important usage of this major-to-minor approach is in helping to define the very important yet subtle differences between the I and IV chords. The I contains the major 3rd, but when we use the minor 3rd

against the IV chord, it becomes the 7th for that chord.

Ex. 15 shows some licks and exercises that illustrate these minor-to-major bends in action. They should all be executed with the index finger on the *A-* and *G*-string bends, while the 3rd finger (with the other fingers behind it to help) should be used for the high *E*-string bends. In the case of the index-finger bends, make them a pivot away from you, while a bend on the high *E* string should obviously go towards you. Also be sure to practice these enough so that your fingers get used to just how far they should push the string, and that they become accustomed to the difference between the way these bends feel and the way a more common two-note bend feels.

There you have it. Try to apply these bends to your playing, even if you're not strictly a blues nut. It will surely add more color and character to what you're already doing.

→

Ex. 15

Fingerpicking the blues on electric guitar

■ Fingerstyle and flatpick-and-finger techniques offer some great possibilities for blues guitar improvisation. One of my favorite uses is to set up a bass line, and play lead *over* it. This is a very difficult technique to master, but once you do, you'll impress both yourself and your listeners.

The most difficult hurdle is to create *true* separation between bass and lead notes. Initially, your thumb will probably tend to play a bass note with every lead note. The bottom should be consistent, supporting the lead notes as they fly all over the place—think of your thumb as the "backing band" while your fingers take the spot-

➡

light. The patterns in Ex. 16 will help you get into the swing of things. Notice how there's usually a consistent relationship between the bass and lead notes—three lead notes for every two bass notes, for example, or two for every one. Start slowly, then build up speed as your confidence improves.

More double-stop blues

■ One rarely hears enough about playing blues harmony licks (double-stops). I enjoy throwing these into my playing now and then. They add an element of surprise to a solo or fill, while retaining the blues feel. They often turn people's heads around because few listeners are used to hearing blues licks in harmonized form. I recommend the pick-and-finger method for this style of playing, but if you are strictly a picker, by all means try that approach.

When playing harmonized blues licks, I like to slide double-stops to higher positions. This helps you get around the fingerboard, and it takes you to positions where more double-stops are available. Hammer-on and pull-off techniques are also good for this style, but beware of overcrowded fingers getting in each other's way when they try to hammer on; things can get a little sloppy for the uninitiated. Try the exercises in Ex. 17 slowly at first. Experiment with combining double-stop leads with regular single-note playing—you may surprise yourself, and perhaps even change the way you play.

Ex. 17

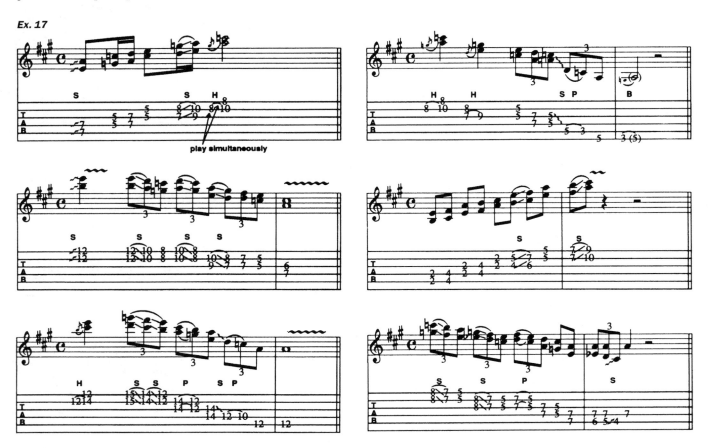

More constant-bass blues

■ Let's continue to explore the soloistic use of constant-bass-with-lead playing. The key to success here is *independence*.

The thumb plays with a shuffle feel throughout Ex. 18. The lead notes parallel the bass, or play the three notes implied by the two shuffle-feel bass notes. Perfecting the three-notes-over-two technique is essential for getting a handle on this type of playing.

Hammer-ons and pull-offs are helpful as the lead pat-terns become more complex. In fact, the actual finger-picking can remain fairly simple, and the rhythm of your picking hand is not so disrupted that it interferes with the constant bass pattern. The end result sounds more complex than it really is, and all the left-hand theatrics let your right hand focus on the rhythm that it must hold down.

Finally, it might be a good idea to learn the lead part first, and then try to slip in the constant bass below it.

➡

Ex. 18

Mastering the I-IV

■ The crucial movement between I and IV at the beginning of a 12-bar blues gives you an opportunity to display your creativity and mastery of the idiom. Let's look at some ideas that enable you to solo over this progression more effectively.

One of the most important notes in I-IV improvisation is the I chord's ♭3rd, which is also IV's ♭7th. This ♭3/♭7 relationship can be utilized in chromatic runs, half-step bends, double-stops, and many other situations, enabling

you to get through the I-IV transition with class and finesse. The ♭3/♭7 concept, combined with IV's ♮3 and other notes, offers many possibilities.

The licks in Ex. 19 are based on the first two measures of a 12-bar blues in the key of *A* and lead back to I. Each exercise has a different "point of view" and should be practiced at a variety of tempos. Once you've absorbed these ideas, experiment and put your personal touch on this great musical moment.

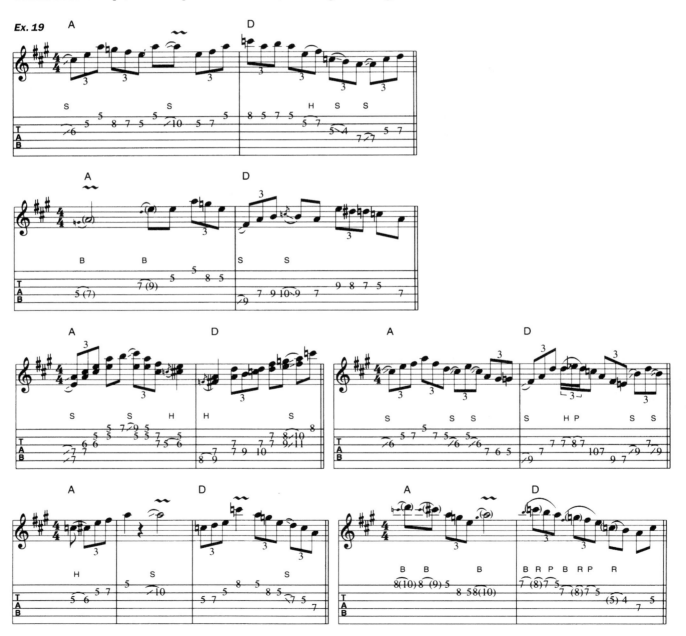

Blue side of country

■ This lesson could just as easily be called "Country side of blues," since the two styles are so intermingled. With a mere shift of attitude and style, bluesy phrasing and tonality can be applied to country-based licks, and country positions can be transformed into bluesier-sounding runs.

In the solo in Ex. 20, observe the pedal steel-like double-stops that incorporate the root and a whole-step bend up to the ♮3rd, as in bar 1's second beat. You can produce a lot of different sounds by relocating this position within the chord/scale structures.

I've used double-stops throughout the solo to reinforce the country effect. Even if you're a hard-core blues player, these techniques can add a lot of diversity and help you avoid the ruts that we all tend to get stuck in from time to time.

Ex. 20

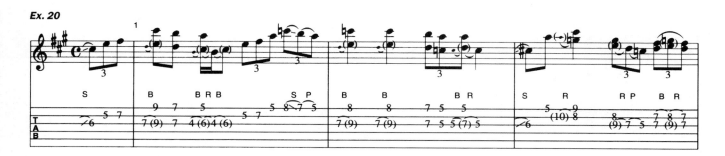

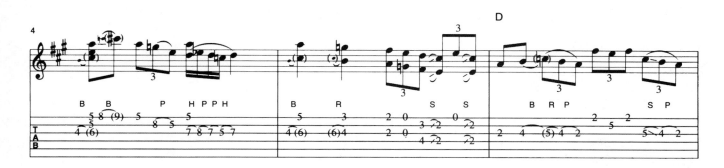

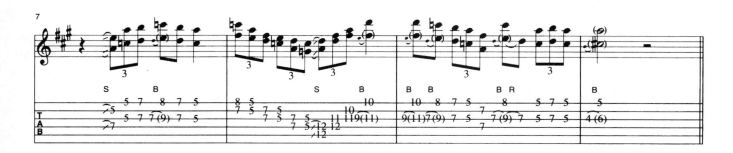

Squealing open strings

■ Blues guitar is on the rise, of course, and its influence resounds everywhere from early rock and roll to heavy metal. In fact, most metal styles are based upon blues. In listening to some of this music, though, I've found that many lead players seem to ignore the emotional and technical possibilities that lie so conveniently within the open positions. This is, after all, where the guitar can really roar and growl with haunting, mysterious sounds. Open-position notes can be dramatically altered simply by changing *where* you pick—near the bridge or neck—

and by *how* you pick. By pinching the pick, for instance, so that flesh and plastic strike the string simultaneously, you can really dig in on low-end licks and create the "false harmonic" squeal sound favored by players like Billy Gibbons of ZZ Top.

The runs in Ex. 21 are based on the open *E, A,* and *D* positions. Notice their differences and similarities, and take advantage of the effect of the ringing open strings. Pay special attention to how the open-string notes fall within the licks. And remember, let it wail!

Ex. 21

Ex. 21 continued

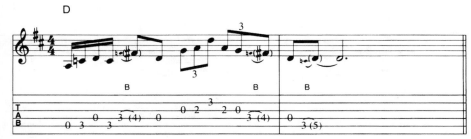

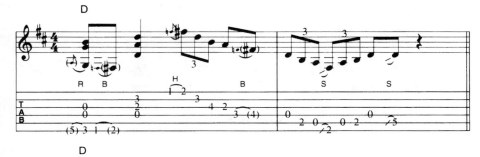

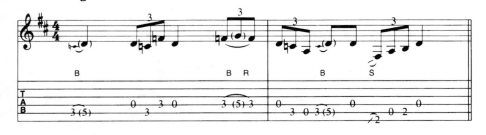

Got the farewell blues

■ Yes, it's true–I really do have the farewell blues, for with this piece, *Hot Guitar* comes to an end. As a parting gesture, I've prepared a rather elaborate piece for you to tackle. I've fittingly entitled it "Farewell Blues," but you'll see that it's blues the way I have always seen it: taking lots of chances, working in country licks, and generally trying to shake up the medium while remaining true to its heart and soul.

Remember folks, play it with feeling, and make every note count.

Ex. 22